Sewing Sculpture

Sewing Sculpture

by Charleen Kinser

M. EVANS AND COMPANY, INC.
New York, New York 10017

M. Evans and Company titles are distributed in
the United States by the J.B. Lippincott Company,
East Washington Square, Philadelphia, PA 19105;
and in Canada by McClelland & Stewart Ltd.,
26 Hollinger Road, Toronto M4B 3G2, Ontario

Library of Congress Cataloging in Publication Data

Kinser, Charleen.
  Sewing sculpture.

  1. Sewing. 2. Soft sculpture. I. Title.
TT715.K56   746.4   76-56736
ISBN 0-87131-215-8
ISBN 0-87131-236-0 pbk.

Design by Charleen Kinser
Manufactured in the United States of America

9 8 7 6 5 4 3 2 1

To Mama, with delightful memories of Belinda, a first-rate muslin doll.

I wish to express my appreciation to the following individuals and companies for their gracious assistance: Purex Corporation for the sock dolls, page 16; The Seven-Up Company for the poster, page 16; Mr. and Mrs. James Cole for Sweet Georgia Sun, page 17; B. Shackman and Company for the silk-screened rabbit, page 25; The Stendig Company for the photograph of the chair, page 62; Dover Publications, Inc., N.Y., for the photograph of the chair, page 63, from The Art Deco Style by Theodore Menten; Robert Keeling for the photograph of the Fairy Godmother, page 82; Chicago Tribune New York News Syndicate, Inc. for the Orphan Annie Dolls, page 125; John Guidaboni for posing with the Bear, page 89; Robert Guidaboni for demonstrating the Seal Slider, page 90; and my other model, Maggie Kinser. Very special thanks to William Ammerman for photographic consultation, and to The Stearns and Foster Company for their generosity in supplying the Mountain Mist polyester Fiberloft for most of the examples in this book.

Contents

Introduction

SEWN SCULPTURE is not a popular art in the same sense that comics are popular, nor can it be a fine art in the modern sense, for when it aims at the high seriousness of what Tom Wolfe calls "the painted word," or at the irony of Pop Art, it is merely pretentious or cute. It cannot escape into the realm of ideas — statements about statements, or art for art's sake. Fine art today is meant to astound, or to express ideas about art. We can't be in awe of sewn sculpture.

Sewn sculpture at its best is a traditional art; both craft (useful and beautifully constructed), and art (delight in form and symbol), or, as Robert Graves describes traditional art: "Art (ars in Latin) is connected with the Greek word artao, to 'join together,' meant in fact what we now call craft in the sense of 'smith-craft' or handicraft. . . ." By this definition, sewn sculpture is also a folk art, which developed out of our ease with the simple craft of sewing and our familiarity with the materials.

Cloth is as natural a sculpture medium to us as stone, wood, or ivory have been or are still to other cultures. Cloth and related materials are a part of our everyday life, just as sealskin and ivory are a part of the everyday life of the Eskimo, who naturally makes utilitarian objects from materials that are close at hand. And since they are common materials with which he is intimately familiar, he uses them just as naturally for his art — beautifully crafted, pocket-sized objects to bring luck in a hunt, or to tell a tale of spirits or men. If you chiseled three planes in a walrus tusk and put it on a pedestal in a museum, we might call it art. But to an Eskimo it would be much ado over a walrus tusk — meaningless, or maybe funny. Carve it into a figure of symbolic importance, and do this beautifully, and he might admire it even while he recognized the walrus tusk.

If we lived as closely with wood, for example, as most Americans did two hundred years ago, we would naturally use wood for our artistic expressions. If you or I or someone in the immediate family cut the trees to make our houses and barns, we would learn the natures of woods. We would make our tables and chairs, carve a wooden spoon, a banister, an ax handle, or a doll's head. And anyone very good at the craft might as naturally carve a symbolic decoration for the church altar.

Instead, we live in a multimedia world of specialists. We do not cut trees to build our houses or tables or toys. Specialists build these things for us. We live with wood, but it is a relatively foreign material to us; and ivory and sealskin are downright exotic. How easily could we learn about the nature of these materials? Whom might we consult for firsthand information? And where would we find the raw material and tools necessary for our first experiments with the medium? They are not at the neighborhood shopping center.

Cloth is familiar to us. Although we no longer make our own cloth out of necessity, many of us may know someone who spins and weaves cloth; we can see the process from fiber to fabric. We wear cloth. Many of us make our own clothing with our own sewing machines. We furnish our houses with cloth articles, and our children play with homemade cloth toys. Sewing cloth is a part of our everyday lives. The materials and tools for this common craft are familiar and readily available to us. We live intimately with cloth. What material, then, is a more natural medium for our art?

Enjoying the Craft

CONTRARY to our romantic fantasies, inside every human being there is not a genius trying to get out. Genius is a multitude of overlapping, finely synchronized, highly developed talents. You either have it or you don't. If you are over the age of twelve and have no signs of genius yet, you will probably never be great. So relax and enjoy yourself. Enjoy the talents you have and your abilities to use them. There are myriad levels between great and hopeless. You do not need genius to turn out some pretty nice work, even to build a career around it.

Talents in fewer numbers are more easily dealt with. Talents can be exploited through learned skills. The lack of any noticeable talent does not make it hopeless for us to pursue our interests. Some of us with little or no culinary talent who love to cook spend time, energy, and money developing our skills to an admirable level. Some of us with no athletic talents to boast of spend hours in pools and on the courts, grids, diamonds, and courses all the same. The more talented among us go through similar, perhaps intensified agonies and delights developing their skills to greater heights.

It's important to give any natural abilities we might have every opportunity to emerge. Perhaps you have a great color sense, just naturally choosing colors that together are stimulating; or you have an innate sense of drama; you stage details with finesse; you use textures excitingly; you sew easily; or you are highly conscious of symbolism. All of these natural abilities can be of great value in sculptural sewing.

Perhaps, through this book, I can help you appreciate more fully just what it is that you now do instinctively as you work, so that you can use your natural abilities or talents to their fullest potential. If you hope to make a career of your craft, perhaps I can help you achieve a little professional distance from your work.

Design is a major consideration throughout this book because design is an integral part of all fine and applied art. Design is not something to do after you are an accomplished craftsman — you can't become one without it. Designing is the craft of combining elements for a particular effect; it can be learned. You combine elements to make a stuffed piece just as you assemble your daily dress or arrange your living room. Whether you design your own initial forms or use an existing pattern, you are designing the moment you begin to collect the elements.

I hope to show you how to look at individual parts and see in them all their potential as design elements. I want you to experience the thrill of seeing a single piece of cloth, for example, as if it were the whole world for a few exciting minutes; to feel its weight, to notice the intricacies of its weave, to sense its nature, and to read its surface patterns and colors, rich with connotations. Combining just two such multifaceted materials is a rich experience, for each facet interacts with all the others. The connotations change. A theme is established. Leaving these interactions to chance is missing the fun of making things.

I hope you'll have such a great time making a sewn sculpture piece that you'll laugh out loud when you do something that delights you. I hope that you will find help, encouragement, and inspiration here when you need it, and that, when your work goes badly, you will recall reading something about unavoidable flops and realize that you're not the only one who has sewed a stuffed disaster, then added button eyes in a frantic attempt to save a week's work. Producing finished pieces is the only way to develop intimacy with a craft — and the doing can be a delightful involvement.

Discovering the Potential of the Craft

SEWN SCULPTURE, as I refer to it in this book, is any sewn form that is stuffed to retain that form. The object may be as utilitarian as a pincushion or as purely aesthetic in value as a piece of sculpture, either naturalistic or nonrepresentational in form.

Each craft has specific inherent qualities that, in the hands of the craftsman or artist, become the tools of expression. Too often the novice follows his enthusiasm into a craft without recognizing its potential or its limitations, which puts him at a great disadvantage. So let's look closely at the inherent qualities, the natural characteristics, of sewn and stuffed sculpture. By becoming aware of these qualities, and of the individual elements that produce them, we can use the craft to its fullest potential.

The Inherent Qualities of Sewn Sculpture

Reality
Like all sculpture, sewn sculpture has spatial reality — three-dimensional form defined by real light and shadow. It has spatial gesture, and real weight, subject to gravity. In addition, sewn sculpture may utilize the colored and tactile surfaces of its materials for their naturalistic qualities.

Three-dimensional Form
The three-dimensional forms of sewn sculpture are predetermined by flat shapes cut from cloth or clothlike materials, and are dependent upon the pliability of those materials.

The surface appearance, the gesture, and the weight of a stuffed sculptural form is greatly influenced by the filling material and the density with which it is packed. Because of the outward pressure of the filler, both concave and flat planes are unnatural to stuffed forms. Flat cloth shapes, when joined and stuffed, become a series of convex planes. Sculpture made up entirely of rounded forms, however, tends to resemble the "rubbery" drawings associated with early animated cartoons. This association can cause the failure of a sculptural statement not intended to be cute or humorous.

Seam Lines
Seams are the inherent linear element in sewn sculpture. They are almost always noticeable; they are therefore considered for more than their structural value. They may be decorative, or strategically placed to delineate three-dimensional form or shape within form.

The visual quality of stitches in cloth carries certain homey connotations difficult to overlook. The type of seam, or quality of line, in a piece of sewn sculpture is an expressive detail.

Varied Surfaces

The wide range of possible surfaces in the craft of sewn sculpture includes the tactile and visual surface qualities of any cloth or related material that is suitable for sewing. By the surface qualities of these materials, the sculptural forms may be given illusions of greater or lesser depth, of movement, of form where there is none, and of naturalism.

The majority of materials commonly used in the creation of sewn sculpture not only are familiar to us but bring associations based on that familiarity. These associations may be utilized to advantage or destroyed by other elements; they cannot be ignored.

The natural characteristics of sewn, stuffed sculpture are present in every piece. The individual elements making up these characteristics are the inherent ones of the craft: three-dimensional form, shape, and gesture, from the original flat shapes, assembled and stuffed; line, from the method of construction; color (hue, value, intensity), pattern, and texture, from the surface materials. When controlled — designed — for a specific effect, these are the tools of expression through which the craft becomes a medium.

Working within the limitations of the materials and techniques of this craft, we find we can sew and stuff just about anything. The question is no longer "Can I do it?" but "Should I do it? Will the inherent qualities of this craft medium enhance my idea?"

My Criteria for a Successful Sewn Sculpture

Most people may or may not appreciate the subtleties of expertise demonstrated by the craftsmanship in a piece of fine art or folk art. They may or may not fully understand its once fashionable style, its symbolism, or even why the piece attracts them at all. A lasting piece of art has a quality about it to which most of us respond — perhaps because we are all human, with basically similar emotions. It may be that we recognize these similarities in one another through the work we produce.

Millions of objects are made in all sculptural materials by every generation of artists and craftsmen. The fact of their being carved from wood, sewn and stuffed, molded in plastic, or chiseled from stone is not an end in itself. The pieces of lasting interest are often magnificently executed; but they always offer someone's perceptions of his world — perceptions shared or found exciting by others.

When I look at a piece of sewn, stuffed sculpture in a gallery exhibit, I expect to be intrigued at least. Like many other gallery-goers, I am eager to see what other craftsmen and designers and artists are doing. I like to be entertained, delighted, surprised, awed, or even upset by the idea expressed through the work. I do not want it to sit there offering me nothing but the fact of its existence. I understand the process of the craft. I am not there to be amazed by a piece's merely being made or by its being huge or tiny. That's not enough. "See the huge stuffed female figure" is not much of a conceptual statement whether written, sung, or stitched. "The big, beautiful doll is superwoman" might be interesting. It is, at least, a concept.

A successful and lasting piece of art arouses a reaction to its concept rather than to its technique or medium. This is true with all the arts. The medium should enhance the idea. A successful piece of soft sculpture should not call attention to the craft itself except where the fact that the piece is sewn and stuffed cloth is an integral part of the concept.

I want to respect the craftsmanship when I finally notice it. An audience is usually eager to see all possible good in a piece of work, but should not be expected to guess what the artist had in mind. Craftsmanship is an inseparable part even of folk art. The concept is carried through and enhanced by every detail.

Looking at Sewn Sculpture Pieces

You'll have your favorites among sewn sculpture pieces, of course. You'll respond to the idea or the personality of a piece, or to some quality you may be unable to define at first. You'll be intrigued by the complexity of form suggested by even a few simple shapes. You'll delight in materials beautifully combined for visual and tactile excitement alone, or for their likeness to other substances. You'll follow, visually, the decorative trails of stitching. You will become aware of light and shadow as they emphasize the three-dimensional forms and the textural richness within them. You'll marvel at the strange reality of the thing — not a reality from nature, but one of its own: the reality of bulk, form, and gesture.

If your work in this medium is to be successful, you must be able to isolate the parts from the whole and analyze what you see and your responses.

Perhaps, by sharing these comments on some of my own work with you, I can help you sort and arrange your reactions to pieces you examine. My advantage is that I know the concept behind and the goals set for each piece.

Eskimo Doll

It has a certain stoic charm, but a lack of scale leaves this piece (page 13) in the middle, where no really good piece can be. It's neither a doll nor an art object. If I had made the head smaller or the parka larger; if I had made the body smaller or the legs longer; if I had borrowed more from the Eskimos and less from rag dolls or vice versa, it would be a beauty.

As a doll it will outlast all others. It will survive the sandboxes, sidewalks, dirt, and toss games of several generations. It even smells good. As a table piece, the soft cabretta leather and rabbit fur will invite handling, which would be more rewarding if the shapes were as they should be.

Purex Sock Dolls

The lady sock dolls (page 16) were designed for advertising. Strong overtones of homey warmth reach us through the subject matter (they are nice old

EAT ★★★ DRINK UN ★★★ BE MERRY

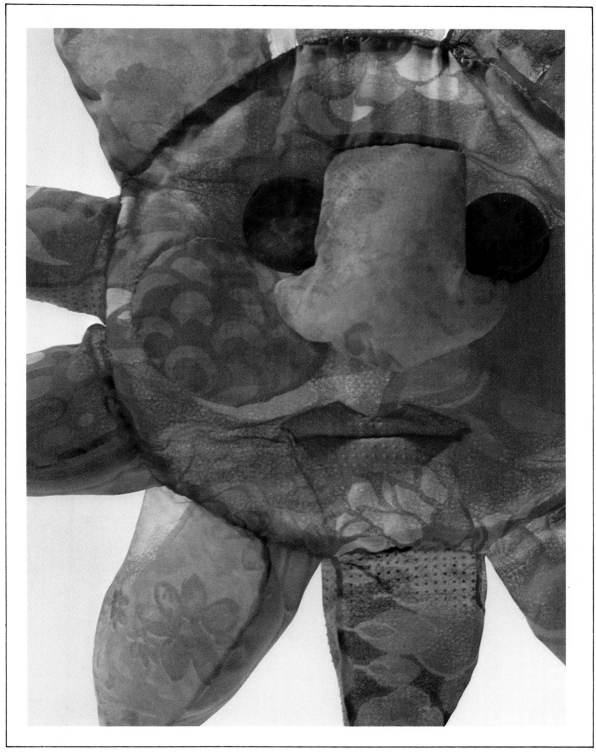

ladies, probably mothers) and through our associations with the old-fashioned sock doll and other homemade dolls. They are two of a charming group of sock dolls, all very friendly and simple, representing a household product — the memory of one supporting the image of the other.

The Pincushion

Triangles and spheres dominate this small piece (page 16), which is truly a design exercise. Spheres and cones are repeated in textures and printed patterns with dots and flowers, diagonal stripes, and triangles, and are accented by a pattern of small squares. The color theme is one of contrasts: black and white and reds, with green and purple accents. Textures include flocked dots and ball fringe, silk acetate, plain and polished cotton. As a pincushion, it's certainly spectacular. It is a playful piece of folk art.

Sweet Georgia Sun

Luminous warm colors filter through the layered surface, an evasive surface created by very sheer fabrics interacting with colored netting fillers (page 17). Metallic eye buttons shine under sheer print coverings. Seam margins that are inside, but visible, become linear accents to the nebulous puffy forms, as if they were drawn outlines.

The face is not the main feature but quietly supports the glowing color theme by association with a sun symbol. This is a playful piece which merely exploits the qualities of the materials.

Game Bird

The piecework and appliqué rendition of a game bird (page 16), designed for purely aesthetic value, has a lifelike bird gesture. Subtle forms provide contrast to a fantasy of luxuriant feather patterns, through intricate woven designs, embroidery, braid, and beads. The piece is exhibited on a branch of compatible color that yet provides a sharp contrast in texture and form.

Upon first glance it is alarmingly realistic. The form supersedes the medium, and that pleases me.

7-Up Hot Dog

The sewn sculpture hot dog (page 16) is an example of the Pop Art of the sixties. It is ironic in that everyday subject matter (the hot dog and 7-Up glass) is treated as art (framed); and doubly ironic in that the Pop Art treatment is then transformed into advertising (made into a poster with a slogan).

The painterly treatment of the bun (clear vinyl painted on the back with acrylics) establishes the "art" connotations in the piece itself. The bread texture is obviously terry cloth. The vinyl sewn-bag mustard rests on a bright-red vinyl wiener. A blue vinyl, star-studded plate provides a dark accent and a platform for the piece and completes the bold, symbolically American color scheme. The entire sewn statement contrasts with and emphasizes the visually delicate real product, 7-Up.

Being an Artist with Your Craft

Developing Visual Awareness

IN THE TRAINING of an artist, great importance is always placed on awareness, or the ability to see relationships in the world for the purpose of making order. The novice sees unselectively, because he looks without purpose. As he becomes involved with a craft, he learns to see the world in terms of that craft. Perhaps at one time you were an avid needlepointer and noticed your increased awareness of subtle colors and textural patterns everywhere, which reminded you of needlepoint stitches. The choreographer sees the world in terms of movement, gesture, rhythmic pattern, and spatial relationships because of his involvement with dance. As a creator of cloth objects, you will see the world in terms of the characteristics of sewn sculpture.

The ability to see relationships is second nature to every good craftsman and professional artist or designer. It is a means of making order, of discovering more than one level of beauty in the world, and of simplifying a concept. It is easy to train yourself to see more selectively, just as you do when you are looking for something in your closet, or for a pin lost in the carpet.

You can learn to see each separate element of an object and to see relationships between the elements as well as between objects. Let me illustrate this by asking you to try a visual exercise that may surprise you. Scan the area around you, noticing the general presence or lack of color. Now think *red,* and look again. Notice every tint of red seeming to come forward, guiding your attention from one area to another like pins on a map. You are discovering color relationships as a means of establishing visual order within an area. Next think *green* and notice how the greens appear where you hadn't noticed them before. Think of any color, even a color you don't expect to find there. If it is present at all, you will see it, perhaps in shadows or highlights.

Look for other types of relationships, using the same exercise; think *pattern, texture, planes,* or *anything round.* Even a messy landscape will appear to take on an orderly quality through the shape and color and texture relationships you are able to see.

To increase your awareness of three-dimensional elements, touch things. Follow contours with your eyes and your hands until you know them. Close your eyes and feel the three-dimensional relationships within an object. Think *round,* and feel all the variations of round (cylindrical, concave, convex, oval, conical) that may be present there. Think *flat,* or *triangular.* Feel the textural relationships, thinking *hairy, ribbed, smooth, knobby.*

As I once suggested to a Brownie troop, hug trees and they'll tell you secrets. If you can get through the sweetness, there's truth in that statement.

Clarifying Your Perception

What you see is yours alone, an image reflecting your personal responses. It is *your* perception. You and I see an actual subject in two different ways. In order for me to react to it in the same or nearly the same way you do, I must perceive it just as you do, which is unlikely, since we are two different people. Therefore, when you see something that so moves you that you want to show me (or others), you must exaggerate or isolate the qualities you want me to notice, and translate them in terms of some medium (sewn sculpture, for example), and in a language of symbols we have in common. Whether expressing your perception of a Kate Greenaway illustration, a gargoyle, or some world situation, the problem is the same: to project your perception in order to stimulate a particular response in someone else. You must first isolate and clarify your perception, then translate it into the terms or elements of your medium, using a language of symbolism you and your audience share.

Awareness of your perceptions is as important to making a successful piece of art as awareness of color or shape, but is probably less often considered by the novice. Look at the photograph below (left) and try to see the subject in a number of different ways. How would you describe the subject in words? How would you emulate it through gestures? What is your perception of the subject? Are the implements diving into the container, or trying to escape from it? Do you notice wood contrasted with crockery? Do you see a comparison between the variety of cylindrical and elliptical forms? Is this *A Pot of Spoons and Things,* or is it *A Collection of Mother's Tools in an Earthenware Crock?*

By thoughtfully isolating and clarifying your perception, you let the subject take on new excitement. See how each different perception seems to change the subject's nature. Who is to say those perceptions are any more or less real than the subject itself? Two often-repeated phrases apply here: "You see what you know about what is there"; and, with a slight shift in emphasis: "How you perceive a thing is what it is."

Since a photographer cannot change the thing itself except by arranging the elements, he selects the light or camera angle to stage the subject in such a way as to direct your attention to the aspects he finds most meaningful. He may only make a dull photograph of cooking utensils, or he may add his point of view and bring you into his picture with your reaction to his *Bouquet,* or *Implements of Culinary Magic.* He might show an explosion of spikes and spears through the use of light and shadows and the focus of his lens and time of the exposure, or the abstraction of the negative shapes within the picture area. He may carefully accentuate the textures and grains of the woods, implying his love for the material, or he may stress the shapes of the individual implements to express his reverence for their variety.

Each of those possibilities is a point of view, a clarified perception. I don't think a successful piece of art, fine or applied, exists without one.

Ideas may come from anywhere and usually come more readily to an inquisitive mind. Ideas may come from emotional reactions to situations or people. They may come from things you see and from things you think you see. They are often inspired by specific problems; for example, my toddler wants a toy toad to take to bed with her; or I need a special touch of yellow on that sofa, or, on a more professional level, the client wants a Pop Art stuffed hot dog (page 16), in which case the problem is to solve the client's problem. Once your idea is clearly perceived, you can begin to express it to others.

Recognizing Symbols

In recent years, a group of prominent graphic designers set out to design a universal language of symbols for use as aids to travelers. Creating graphic symbols for "women" and "men" (clothed) that would be understood worldwide was more difficult than they had imagined, but they convinced themselves and others they had solved the problem with the symbols they chose. Yet restroom signs are still objects of confusion to many world travelers.

Symbolism is perhaps the most difficult of all subjects to discuss because it is infinitely complex. This is, therefore, a simple introduction to symbolism as it relates to sewn sculpture.

Symbols are basic tools of communication. We translate our ideas into one form of symbolism or another in order to convey them to others. In order to reach the intended audience, our ideas must take the form of meaningful symbols for that audience. Anything that has meaning to someone or a group may become a symbol — at least to that person or group. Movement, gesture, shape, form, color, objects, people, plants, words, music, noise, numerals, animals, and groupings are possible symbols.

A single element such as the color red may become the symbol for "hot" or "danger." In combination with a shape symbol, the meaning of the color may change; for example, a red heart shape symbolizes love. Placement of an element may also be symbolic; for example, a red disc on a road map may symbolize the location of a city. A red disc resting on a line may symbolize the setting sun; a red octagon on a stick may symbolize the command to stop. In Christian symbolism, an apple shown in the hands of Adam means sin; in the hands of Christ, it symbolizes the fruit of salvation.

An object or an element may be symbolic of one idea to one group and of an entirely different idea to another group. For example, the serpent in Aztec art represents life; in Christian art it represents evil. The dandelion, a lowly weed to the grass keeper, is a spring treasure to the natural foods enthusiast.

The symbolic language must be understood by its audience. Remember the importance of fashionable symbols in your teen years. Not only the clothing you wore or aspired to wear, but also the gestures and language you used, and where you wished to be seen and doing what, held great symbolic importance. These symbolic elements classified you as a part of a group.

In order to convey an idea through sewn sculpture, you must translate the idea into symbols by means of the elements of the craft: namely, three-dimensional form, gesture, stitches, cloth, color, texture, the subject matter itself, and where and how the finished object is finally placed or used.

As you select materials for your sculpture, you will automatically consider their common symbolic meaning to you and to your group. If you want your piece to be fully appreciated by a particular group you must use symbols in your fabric statement that the group will immediately understand. Burlap, for example, is one thing to a decorator, but something else entirely to a farmer. The larger the intended audience, the more general your symbolism must be. For an audience of friends, your cloth-and-form language can be as intimate as hometown colloquialisms or family idioms.

Cloth, the basic stuff of clothing all these centuries, bears connotations based in cultural beliefs and in fashion. But if cloth is seen for its potential as an element of symbolism in color, texture, and pattern, and not only as clothing material, it becomes an even more versatile material for sewn sculpture.

By means of its textures and colors, cloth has many surface qualities resembling surfaces in nature and therefore may become symbols for those things. You may find hard-finish suiting fabric resembling stone, sand, or bird colorations; white cotton piqué resembling a sun-bleached shell; velvet like a pansy petal, and iridescent blends like butterfly wings.

In addition to its range of naturalistic appearances, cloth used for its texture alone may symbolize a variety of ideas. For example, burlap may become a symbol for rough, rustic, rural; velvet may imply softness, sexiness, royalty; and muslin may symbolize rural, peasant, practical ideas. Pattern symbols may be: challis print for peasant; gingham check for rural; paisley for exotic; large dots for a clown. The color blue may symbolize loyalty, sadness, or cold. Yellow may be the symbol for happy, sunny, or cowardly.

Three-dimensional form and its arrangement are the physical expression of attitude or gesture in a sculptural piece. Forms may symbolize objects as well as ideas; for example, a spiral form may be a symbol for a snail or for inward or outward movement. Form with gesture may symbolize ideas such as: humble — a bowed form; menace — a form with forward thrust; hesitant or shy — a form leaning backwards.

To establish symbolic gestures for the idea you wish to convey, act them out — pose, before a mirror if you wish. In making the Crowd of Ogres (pages 107, 108), for example, think the word symbol *menacing*. Act menacing, and note your body attitude or gesture. Make menacing sounds to arouse your full awareness of the act. Think harder — MENACING. Notice the details of the gesture: outstretched arms, grasping fingers, squinted eyes perhaps. Where are the wrinkles? Where is your body tensed and where is it soft? Try to see and feel the gestures from other views. Try changing *menacing* into a cartoon symbol. Note your comical face, the silliness of the mock gestures.

Symbols differ among cultural, religious, social, economic, racial, occupational, and age groups. The more widely accepted symbols seem to represent the basic emotions and characteristics of mankind such as joy, sorrow, anxiety, greed, anger, triumph, and are expressed through the elements of gesture and shape that people themselves make in expressing these emotions. Much of our symbolism is only fashionable and loses its meaning quickly. The most meaningful symbols to a great many people today are more likely to be somewhat less meaningful to future generations. To make a sewn sculpture piece more lasting in meaning, the idea should be as basic as Aesop's fables, and carried through as widely accepted symbols.

If in the wake of this brief encounter with the subject of symbolism, you are aware that every element in your sewn sculpture (pillows included) is a potential symbol, then you are on your way. Awareness of the symbolism of his own and other groups is essential to an artist.

Recognizing Useful and Inspiring Forms in Sewn Objects and in Nature
We are all familiar with numerous common sewn objects. To a designer/craftsman whose interest is sewn sculpture, these objects are a collection of useful and possibly inspiring forms. As you learn to see more purposefully, and as you gain experience in the craft of three-dimensional sewing, you too will discover sewn sculptural objects — simple objects such as the ones pictured here — for their value to you as a designer. They offer a variety of

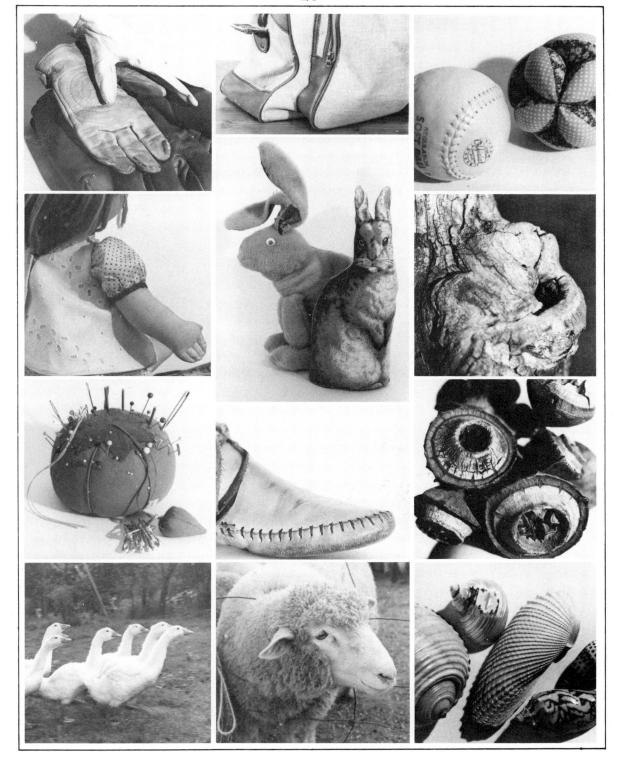

exciting shapes to use in your work: not right away, perhaps, but you'll soon feel ready to put together your own first shapes to see what happens. Many of the problems you would otherwise encounter in making these sculptural forms have been solved already. You probably sew many of these complex forms without thinking of them as being sculpture. Many are common shapes in accessory- and clothes-making.

Your observations will simplify your work. Always try to find the similarities rather than the differences between this sewing craft and other three-dimensional and flat sewing — a good rule to follow as you begin any new craft experience. Simply assume there is nothing new; everything is a variation of what you've seen or done before.

Look closely at all sewn forms for what they may suggest to you. Notice their potential as forms for other objects in other sizes, in combinations, or in repetition. Notice, if you can, the flat shapes that predetermine those three-dimensional forms. Look at toys and overstuffed furniture, clothing parts, and other sewn sculpture. Variations of the shapes you discover will become parts of your sculptural-sewing language.

You will use some of these forms again and again in making pieces from the patterns in this book. The most directly borrowed example is the puff sleeve shape, the basis of the chair pictured on page 68. The Bear (page 89) and the leather Gentlebeast (page 127) have set-in sleeve legs, and the Bear's head is made movable by means of an under-arm gusset at the throat. The Crowd of Ogres (pages 107, 108) has an assortment of head and nose shapes borrowed from footwear and mittens, coin purses and valises. And the toads (page 88) squint through bound buttonhole eyelids.

Try to picture natural forms as sewn and stuffed pieces. How would you translate a particular gnarled tree trunk into cloth forms? Look very closely at a seed pod, picturing the planes of its interior and textured outer hull as cloth forms. What forms do you feel as you stroke a cat? And have you ever held a large bird in its sleek feather case? Picture the great conical and rounded forms in cloth. Look at firm, round flower buds, multi-shaped seashells, and people with their outer shells of clothing. Simple, beautiful, inspiring forms are everywhere — they'll remind you of the rich possibilities of this sculptural craft.

Attitude

There are numerous frustrations built into this craft. You may as well develop the ability to laugh at yourself; your predicaments are bound to amuse someone.

"How nice to be able to create things" — you've heard that many times, no doubt. Hold that thought as you work. Someday you'll be stuffing an ogre or something else, and it will seem to swallow you. You'll put your share of feet on backwards, deform your share of noses, and try to turn a doughnut shape inside out. You'll poke around inside some piece looking for your needle, or finally turn a tricky shape right side out only to find the foam backing on the outside after all your careful planning. Worse still, you will one day bring to a magnificent finish an inspired piece of soft sculpture and someone will say, "Oh, how cute."

Most problems can be solved, most errors can be corrected, and starting over is not as awful as you may imagine. Depressing as they are, errors have their value: they are not easily forgotten. The more varied your experiences with the craft, the greater your collection of things to avoid — and your number of successes. Experience and success lead to confidence, that elusive and vital tool. Most craft skills and all creative art skills are developed through a great deal of practice and a sincere involvement, and not without some emotional pain. That widely agreed upon fact may comfort you through your first stuffed disaster.

Give yourself the pleasure, the exhilaration of total involvement in your work — and at the same time, try to develop a sensible perspective. "Sensible perspective" refers to the ability to pull back, out of your sensitive and total involvement, and become practical, or less emotionally involved, now and then. As you select materials, for example, you should enjoy yourself completely, following your inner reactions to the fabrics. But then a moment of detached appraisal is in order. A sensible perspective gives you the distance needed to foresee problems that might later ruin some otherwise great afternoon at the sewing machine. Each part of a sewn sculpture is dependent on every other part, all of which are preplanned in the earliest stages. In sewn sculpture, very few surprises turn out to be pleasant ones.

Each time you produce in any art or craft, you progress one step from the work you produced last. Each piece of work will be a little more exciting to a few more people, a little better made, and done not only with more ease but with deeper understanding of the craft. It doesn't matter how long you wait between one effort and the next, or how much you think you've changed — one step is all you can hope for. "Sensible perspective" means realizing this, and not expecting more of yourself than you can do. The ability to bring together numerous elements in a piece of work, beautifully, develops slowly, with practice, in arts and crafts as in every other endeavor. Unfortunately your critical ability seems to grow to some degree whether or not you produce; so when you do work again, your other skills take only that one step and the more highly developed critic in you can't stand it. You become discouraged, and the work is completed without spirit or success, or it is left unfinished.

Allow yourself to accept utter defeat with ease and grace and begin another piece. There is pain of sorts in making personal statements through art. Sometimes it's frightening. It takes courage to express a viewpoint in a concrete piece of work. You can't follow it up with, "What I meant is . . ."

One day you'll be working and everything will fall into place beautifully, the next day everything will turn to frayed seams and puckers. There is always the sewing machine to blame, or the gravitational pull of the moon, or some planet in some astrological house. But there is one very logical explanation: yesterday you were gathering together all you had previously struggled to learn; today you are trying to take the next step — and a new struggle begins.

Set your goals as high as you dare for each piece of work. Then, as single-mindedly as possible, set out to achieve your goals. Try to resist compromises, even at the risk of failure. Start again if necessary and strive to develop the skills and sensitivity needed to achieve something near your original aspirations. Please yourself; delight yourself — if you can, for you should be your most severe critic. You are the only one who knows what you tried to do.

If you want to try something, do it wholeheartedly, right out there in cloth, where you can see if it works or not. Don't slide into some easier compromise. No failure is more difficult to bear than failing to try.

The Professional
The professional artist, craftsman, and designer differs from the nonprofessional only in his greater experience, confidence, and ability to be objective about his work. He must be able to approach a commissioned piece of work, often the client's idea, with enthusiasm, and, in the commercial field, be willing to make alterations in a piece or begin again at the client's request. In the fine art field, he may enter his personal work in craft or art shows, or exhibit it in a gallery for the purpose of selling it. He may even be commissioned to do a piece of work of his choice by some private collector.

The degree of professionalism you attain with experience will allow you to develop objectivity toward your work, isolate your feelings, and clarify your reactions toward subject matter, materials, and all other aspects of a piece of work. You will develop enough distance to use or set aside a particular material because of whether or not it suits the project, regardless of whether it is your favorite color or print or texture. You will find your list of favorites becoming longer. When they are used well in a piece of work, all colors and fabrics have a certain beauty.

Background and Preparation

The Natures of the Materials

THE PHYSICAL nature of a piece of cloth is dependent upon its fiber content and upon the method by which it is made. An extensive knowledge of cloth fabrics and their fiber contents is not a prerequisite for making soft sculpture. By feeling cloth, you can usually guess how it will react to sewing and stuffing. You may rumple it in a warm hand for a few moments to see if it wrinkles excessively or goes limp with handling. You may scratch a small corner to test the durability of its surface. You may read the manufacturer's instructions for its care. But in order to use a piece of fabric to the fullest advantage, without any surprises in the process, you should acquaint yourself with the physical qualities of its fibers and structure.

Fibers and Fabrics

Fibers are the individual units or strands that are spun together to make yarn. Natural fibers come from plants such as cotton and flax; from animals such as sheep, goats, and camels; or from the silkworm. In addition to natural fibers, there is a growing list of synthetic fibers made from such sources as wood, glass, metal, rubber, and chemicals.

COTTON is the most commonly used fiber in the textile industry. There are numerous qualities and varieties of cotton fibers, used to produce cloth in a wide range of weights, strengths, and textures; all are easy to work with. Cotton cloth is a versatile and inexpensive material for soft sculpture. It is washable and easily dyed and may be bleached. It must be ironed.

LINEN fibers, among the strongest natural fibers, differ widely in their qualities and are classed accordingly for making various fabrics ranging from rough sacking to the most delicate sheers. Linen cloth has a hard finish that makes it more soil- and moisture-resistant than cotton cloth. Linen may be either washed or dry-cleaned. It takes dye well, but is damaged by chlorine bleach.

Of all the commercially available animal-hair fabrics, WOOL is the only one I consider suitable for use in soft sculpture. It is the most durable and the least expensive of the animal fibers.

WOOL fiber comes from the fleece of sheep and produces a luxurious and resilient yarn. Wool is made into cloth in a limited range of weights and finishes and is often blended with other fibers. Some wool blends are washable and should be pressed using a press cloth. All pure woolen fabric should be dry-cleaned. Lint and dust can be removed with a lint brush or vacuum cleaner. The only real disadvantage of wool is its susceptibility to moth damage; but many wool fabrics are pretreated against moths.

Wool fabric labeled *virgin wool* is made from wool yarn that contains no fibers from reclaimed knits or fabrics. Virgin wool may be molded to take a form, making it an exciting soft sculpture medium. If well protected from moths, it will last several generations.

A fabric called *reprocessed wool* is made from reclaimed virgin wool scraps. It is less durable and not as strong or resilient as virgin wool.

Wool fabric simply labeled *wool* is made from yarn containing virgin wool fibers as well as reclaimed fibers from knits. It is less durable and less resilient than virgin wool.

SILK is a luxurious fiber produced by the caterpillar of the moth *Bombyx mori,* a domesticated insect raised for its silken cocoons.

Silk fabrics are made in a number of textures, from smooth to knobby, and in varied weights. They are all resilient and extremely strong. If its price is acceptable to you, silk is a good candidate for soft sculpture pieces because of its durability and variety. Silk is hand-washable with mild soap and takes dye well. Only hydrogen peroxide or sodium perborate bleaches should be used on silk.

Among the fabrics produced from synthetic fibers, those most suitable for sewn and stuffed pieces are made from or contain acrylic, nylon, or polyester fibers.

ACRYLIC fabrics are crease-resistant, resilient, and washable, but they are also bleach-resistant and heat-sensitive. Orlon (one of the acrylic fiber trademarks) is often blended with wool or cotton, as is Acrilan (another trademark). They are washable and bring that quality to wool/Acrilan and wool/Orlon blends. You may mold or shape acrylic fabrics to some degree while they are still warm from ironing.

MODACRYLICS (modified acrylics) are the fibers used in such materials as fake fur. They are extremely sensitive to heat. They may be gently washed if necessary in cool water, tumble-dried, and ironed damp on the wrong side, using the lowest temperature setting. It is wise to consult the manufacturer's instructions for the care of fake fur fabrics.

NYLON fibers are incredibly strong, elastic, and dirt-resistant. When blended with other fibers, they produce fabrics with those qualities. Nylon and nylon-blend fabrics are produced in many finishes and weights. All are washable and dry quickly but are heat-sensitive. Nylon should be ironed on the wrong side with a very low temperature setting if pressing is required.

POLYESTER fiber is perhaps the most springy, resilient, and wrinkle-resistant of all fibers. Polyester, often blended with natural fibers, is made into a variety of minimum-care fabrics as well as batting and sewing thread. These fabrics are washable and are not harmed by chlorine bleach. They dry quickly and require little or no ironing. Dacron, Fortrel, Kodel, and Vycron are trademarks for polyester fiber.

All cloth is made from fibrous yarns that are either woven, knitted, or felted (fused) together.

WOVEN FABRICS are made from vertical "warp" yarns that are interwoven with horizontal "weft" or weaving yarns. The great variety of textures and finishes found in woven cloth is the result of combinations of yarns and of warping and weaving patterns. The finished edges created by the weft are called selvages.

The vertical and horizontal pattern of warp and weft yarns is referred to as the "grain" of the fabric, with the warp indicating the lengthwise grain. A 45-degree-angle through this grain is called the "bias." In woven fabrics, the bias is the only direction in which there is any noticeable stretch, or "give."

KNITTED FABRICS have a lengthwise rib created by the knit stitch. The greatest degree of stretch is across the rib pattern, not on the bias angle as in woven fabric. Many knits have the quality of woven fabrics, or little noticeable stretch. They are called firm, stable, and bonded (made stable by a bonded backing) knits. The degree of stretch in knits is far-ranging, as is the number of textures and finishes. Raschel and rough-textured, medium-firm knits are firm, but not rigid. Sweater, loose, and stretchable knits stretch freely in both directions like hand knits. Single, thin, and supple knits have a moderate to maximum crosswise stretch and a moderate lengthwise stretch.

In addition to these groups, there are furry-faced knits, shiny-faced knits, stretch terry, lingerie knits, and spandex stretch knits, each with its own stretch characteristics.

FELTED FABRICS are made of fibers that are interlocked by pressure, beating, moisture, and heat — the oldest method of cloth making. True felt is made from wool fibers, sometimes combined with fur or hair. It is somewhat springy and may be stretched or molded over a form. Felt is not a very strong or durable fabric.

G.M.L. (GENUINE MILLED LEATHER) is a material with pulverized leather fused to a cloth backing. It is sometimes dyed in leather tones. It may be sponged, hand-washed, or dry-cleaned.

Leathers, Furs, and Fleece

Leather is the most durable material you can choose for soft sculpture, and perhaps the most versatile. One or another type of leather may be sewn and stuffed, laminated, soaked and molded over a form, or stretched over an armature. It may be dyed, bleached, painted, embossed or tooled, batiked, burned, carved, or embroidered.

There are two principal tanning methods that transform animal hides and small animal skins into leather: vegetable tanning, a two- to six-month process using tree bark extracts, and chrome tanning, a one-day process using soluble chromium salts. Vegetable-tanned leather absorbs moisture. It is the only leather suitable for tooling and stamping, since those forms of ornamentation require thoroughly dampened leather. Vegetable-tanned leather is used extensively in making shoe soles, harnesses, luggage, and upholstery. Chrome-tanned leather is water-resistant and is primarily used for shoe uppers, garments, and accessories such as gloves and handbags.

Small animal skins such as calf, goat, lamb, rabbit, or pig are usually sold as whole skins. Large animal skins may be purchased as whole *hides,* or by the *side* (one half hide, lengthwise), the *back* (choice, upper part of a side), or the *belly* (lower part of a side). Leather is priced by the square foot. A whole cowhide usually measures from 42 to 50 square feet; a calf skin, from 9 to 15 square feet. An average pig skin measures from 5 to 8 square feet.

Experienced eyes and hands grade the leather 1, 2, 3, 4, and so on, or A, B, C, D, and so on. Grade does not refer to quality but denotes the degree of perfection of the surface. Grade 1, or A, identifies an almost perfect hide, the imperfections being smaller than the size of a hand; grade 2, or B, indicates imperfections equal to the size of two hands. The scratches, small holes, brand marks, stains, and other imperfections of a lower-grade hide are not necessarily undesirable in sculpture.

The weight of a specific leather indicates its thickness and is determined by the weight of one square foot of that leather. One-ounce leather is approximately 1/64 inch thick. The weights, all applicable to one sculptural form or another, range from 1 to 14 ounces, 14-ounce being used for sling and strap furniture. Garment-weight leather is generally between 1 and 4 ounces and may be sewn on most home sewing machines.

Leather will stretch but does not shrink from its original size. Its greatest strength is in the center and with the grain, or parallel to the backbone. Some degree of stretch occurs in most leathers at the belly area and at right angles to the grain.

Suedes may be brushed clean with a suede brush or fine sandpaper. To clean smooth-grained leathers, apply saddle soap with a wet sponge, lather, wipe off with a dry cloth, then polish.

Store leather away from heat, which dries it out; sunlight, which fades it; and moisture, which may cause mold. Roll it flesh side out and wrap it in brown paper, lay it flat, or drape it over a rod to hang freely.

The following are a few of the most commonly available leathers: buckskin: deer and elk with the grain removed; cabretta: Brazilian hair sheep; calfskin; capeskin: South African sheep; cowhide; deerskin: deer and elk; goatskin; hair calf: calfskin with the hair intact; hair sheep: sheep species with hairlike wool; horsehide; kidskin; kipskin: an intermediate-size cow or steer, larger than a calf; lambskin: lamb with wool removed; latigo: oil-tanned cowhide; live oak: cowhide specially tanned for tooling and sculpture; pigskin; Pigtex and Pecca Pig: trade names for lambskin embossed to resemble pigskin; Shearling: sheepskin tanned with the wool on; sheepskin; skiver: the grain layer split from a sheepskin.

The less commonly available leathers include: alligator; kangaroo; lizard; ostrich; peccary: wild boar from Central and South America; sealskin; sharkskin; snake; walrus; and water buffalo.

Most of the exotic leather grains listed are available in embossed cowhide at much lower prices.

I will not attempt to describe the myriad textures, patterns, and colors offered by the skins of fur-bearing animals, except that they range from long, straight monkey fur to short, curly Persian lamb; from zebra stripes to leopard spots. The only fur I have found commonly available at the retail level is rabbit, and it is the only fur represented in the soft sculpture in this book.

It is best to have fur dry-cleaned by specialists, who use cleaning solvent on finely ground tropical nutshells. Hang fur over wooden or padded coat hangers or rods, in paper or cloth bags, never in plastic. Fur requires constantly circulating cool air to prevent the skin from drying out.

Vinyls

As applicable here, vinyls are available as transparent and translucent yard goods and tubing, and as coated cloth. Although vinyl coating tends to crack and peel under heavy use, it offers a uniquely slick surface quality or even transparency to sewn sculpture. Vinyls may be painted with acrylics or tinted with strong dyes.

Threads and Yarns for Utility and Ornament

Threads naturally carry the characteristics of their fiber content and are made of nearly all the common textile industry fibers.

Thread (and yarn) has a smooth and a rough direction that you can feel by holding one end and sliding your lightly pinched thumb and forefinger of the other hand in one direction the length of the thread, and then in the opposite direction. The thread will feel smooth as your fingers move toward the spool (or skein), and rough moving

away from the spool. For trouble-free sewing with fewer tangles, always thread the needle with the end of the thread that comes first from the spool (diagram a) and retain that needle position as you sew.

MERCERIZED COTTON thread is *the* most congenial thread for hand sewing. Mercerizing is a lustrous permanent finish applied to some cotton fabric and thread.

LINEN thread is smoother, more lustrous, and slightly heavier than cotton thread, with twice the strength.

SILK is a very high-gloss, twisted thread that is extremely smooth and difficult to keep from tangling. It is luxurious, durable, and expensive.

NYLON thread is the strongest sewing thread. It is too strong for use with delicate fabric: the cloth will tear before the thread will break. Its flexibility makes it ideal for stretch fabrics. Nylon thread is completely unwieldy for hand sewing, and not the most congenial machine thread. It is at its most cooperative after being lightly steamed over a teakettle.

POLYESTER thread has become the new all-purpose sewing thread by surpassing the strength and resilience of cotton thread.

The decorative cotton, wool, silk, linen and even metallic threads of surface stitchery are equally ornamental for sewn sculpture; and those of durable fibers may be used in stitching seams.

An astounding number of bulky, nubby, lustrous, and hairy yarns used in knitting, crocheting, rug hooking, and weaving are also possible additions to soft sculpture.

Fillers

Filling materials are made from many of the fibers used in cloth-making. The nature of the fiber indicates the nature of the filling material, or batting, as it is called. Batting is a fluff of fibers sold loose in bags or, in some fibers, rolled into sheets for use in quilts.

COTTON batting tends to wad or lump and has less resilience than other batting.

POLYESTER batting is extremely resilient and retains a form well.

DOWN, breast feathers from the eider duck, is extremely soft and resilient. Down is expensive and not readily available.

FOAM RUBBER and POLYURETHANE FOAM in sheets, cubes, spheres, and cylinders of various sizes, thicknesses, and densities are indispensable where a flat or smooth surface is desired. Shredded, they provide a highly resilient, bumpy surface.

STYROFOAM PELLETS, extremely lightweight, shift position and squeak a little.

In addition to commercially prepared fillers, a few natural fibrous materials are suitable for stuffing sewn sculpture, some being even more desirable because of the textural qualities they provide.

EXCELSIOR is a tangle of thin wood shavings that compacts to make a firm, lightweight filling. It provides an interesting texture and sound.

DRIED GRASSES and STRAW, probably the oldest stuffing materials, offer a rustling sound and an irregular texture to sewn sculpture. They should be thoroughly dried and sprayed with an insecticide before use.

WOOD SHAVINGS and SAWDUST tend to shift, altering the sewn form. Wood shavings, especially cedar shavings, have a pleasant aroma.

SAND and PEBBLES add weight to soft sculpture. They shift inside a sewn form, changing the shape.

Any soft, resilient, fibrous SCRAPS from sewing, stitchery, or knitting make inexpensive fillers.

AROMATIC MATERIALS such as crushed dried flowers, herbs, or even tobaccos are not only a delight to use but add an unexpected element to a sewn sculpture.

(a)

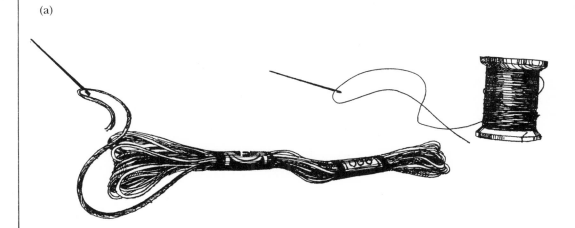

Collecting Materials

Sewn sculpture materials are those designed primarily for clothing, accessories, or interior decorating. As fashions in clothing and decorating change, certain materials drift in and out of vogue.

The textile industry follows the trends closely, making some fabrics difficult to find only a few months after their introduction. A few seasons ago, for example, fashion induced the increased production of calico prints, renaming them "granny" prints. They appeared on nearly every type of cloth for one or two seasons. Then, as suddenly, tie-dye became the new fashion image. If you had just decided to make a piece of sewn sculpture using granny prints, you would have had very little selection.

The fashionable colors vary from one summer or winter to the next. Even the basic reds, yellows, blues, and greens, as they are applied to any but the most standard cloth, differ in character from season to season. The most subtle difference can alter the personality of a color, and our reactions to it change with the fashion. A good collection of remnants from different seasons will give you a greater selection of colors, prints, and textures.

Some fascinating materials are often found in unlikely places. Resale shops and rummage or garage sales often have draperies, spreads, quilts, blankets, coats, furs, leather articles, and outdated but nearly new clothing made of the fabrics of yesteryear. Variety stores and even your least favorite discount department stores usually carry a stimulating selection of near-miss fabrics bought as mill ends of discontinued designs. Antique shops often have quilts, carpets, shawls, and fancy linens that are still useful as cloth for soft sculpture. (The Game Bird, page 16, is made from an old paisley shawl scrap.)

Leather is available through mail order and, in some areas, retail craft and leathercraft stores. The local shoemaker may be able to help you locate leather suppliers. Custom leatherwork shops often sell their scraps. The owner or buyer may generously consent to purchase a piece of leather for you from his wholesaler. That would be a special kindness and should be regarded as such — don't march in expecting that kind of help.

Resale shops often have leather articles that may be taken apart, cleaned, and re-used successfully. Some otherwise unobtainable types of leather may be found in used articles.

Sheep and rabbit skins are available through some leather supply stores and mail order houses. Other animal furs are not commonly available except as trims in some fabric shops. But resale shops often have a selection of furs and fur-trimmed articles of clothing or fur rugs.

Sources for Supplies

Batik Supplies

Aljo Manufacturing, 116 Prince Street, New York, N.Y. 10012
Batik Craft Supplies, 1 Industrial Road, Woodbridge, N.J. 07075
Saks Arts and Crafts, 1103 North Third Street, Milwaukee, Wis. 53203
Macmillan Arts and Crafts, Inc., 9520 Baltimore Avenue, College Park, Md. 20740

Down

Frostline Kits, Dept. C, 452 Burbank, Broomfield, Colo. 80020
Worldwide Bedding Shop, P.O. Box 9697, Seattle, Wash. 98109

Fake Fur

Norwood Mills, Inc., 49 West 37th Street, New York, N.Y. 10018

Robbie Robinson Textile Corp., 270 West 39th Street, New York, N.Y. 10018

Fur

Pollack's Furrier's Supply Corp., 160 West 29th Street, New York, N.Y. 10001

The Singer Fur Co., 190 North State St., Chicago, Ill. 60601

Fur Trimmings

Arco Novelty Co., 209 West 26th Street, New York, N.Y. 10001

Leather and Leatherwork Supplies

Berman Leather Co., 145-147 South Street, Boston, Mass. 02111

Macmillan Arts and Crafts: listed under Batik Supplies

Tandy Leather Company, P.O. Box 791, Fort Worth, Tex. 76101

Needlework Supplies

Herrschners, Hoover Road, Stevens Point, Wis. 54481

Merribee Needlecraft Company, 2904 West Lancaster, P.O. Box 9680, Forth Worth, Tex. 76107

Stuffing Materials

Herrschners: listed under Needlework Supplies

Merribee Needlecraft Company: listed under Needlework Supplies

Useful Books

Leatherwork

Grant, Bruce. *Leather Braiding.* Cambridge, Md.: Cornell Maritime Press, Inc., 1961.

Newman, Thelma R. *Leather As Art and Craft.* New York: Crown Publishers, Inc., 1973.

Schwebke, Phyllis W., and Krohn, Margaret B. *How to Sew Leather, Suede, Fur.* New York: Collier Books, Macmillan Publishing Co., 1966.

Wollcox, Donald. *Modern Leather Design.* New York: Watson-Guptill Publications, 1969.

Needlework

Kinser, Charleen. *Personally Yours: Needlepoint.* New York: Consolidated Book Publishers, 1975.

Snook, Barbara. *Needlework Stitches.* New York: Crown Publishers, Inc., 1963.

Thomas, Mary. *Mary Thomas's Embroidery Book.* New York: William Morrow and Co., 1936.

Batik and Dyeing

Adrosko, Rita J. *Natural Dyes and Home Dyeing.* New York: Dover Publications, Inc., 1961.

Meilach, Dona Z. *Contemporary Batik and Tie-Dye.* New York: Crown Publishers, Inc., 1973.

Nea, Sara. *Batik.* New York: Van Nostrand Reinhold Co., 1971.

A Place to Work

You should have a place where you can freely follow the dictates of your projects, without concern for the mess you will make or the inconvenience the accumulation of materials may cause you or others in the house. I know, from years of clearing away my fabrics each mealtime, that the dining room table is not the best cutting surface; but it will do. And from the miles I have hauled supplies, I know just how "portable" a sewing machine is. Although I *can* work in any quiet place, a private refuge is more pleasurable. Whatever you require in the way of privacy, you should have space to spread out your work, excellent light, and some degree of physical and emotional comfort. Beyond that, a working area is such a personal place, I can't prescribe your needs.

I like white walls that don't interfere with color selections I might be making, and since I like to see sketches, notes, pattern shapes, and fabric samples all together as I work, one wall surface must take the abuse of masking tape and pushpins.

Bare floors are easy to sweep and provide a great cutting surface for large pieces. If you're not comfortable working on the floor, a large table or facsimile is a necessity. A piece of smooth ¾-inch plywood, 4 feet by 8 feet, on sawhorse-type legs, and waist-high, makes a good all-purpose table. I stand or use a high stool, as the work dictates.

A lamp with blue and yellow fluorescent tubes can provide simulated daylight, enabling you to see color accurately at night and on gray days.

The hours spent at the sewing machine must be comfortable ones. I use an old bentwood chair, chosen for its height in relation to the sewing machine and me.

A full-length mirror will help you see a piece of work with more distance; and problems are more noticeable in the reverse image. Adjusting shapes, stuffing, or attaching pieces in front of a mirror enables you to see another view of the area in question.

Storage space is a problem I have given up trying to solve. Clear plastic boxes, shelves to the ceiling, chests, and plastic bags will always add their clutter to my work area; and I'm not certain that is altogether undesirable, for the materials of this craft are lovely and a constant source of inspiration to me.

Tools of the Craft

The basic hand tools and sewing aids useful in this craft are those of dressmaking: namely, dressmaker's pins, tailor's chalk or other marking medium, shears, an assortment of sewing-machine and hand-sewing needles, thimbles, a seam ripper, an iron, a pressing cloth and mitt, and a tailor's ham. In addition, you may need some tools for leatherwork (page 51). Any additional tools needed for a specific project in this book are listed with the instructions.

Sewing Machines

Any simple sewing machine in good working condition will suffice. If you have a machine with an assortment of fancy stitches, you will certainly find applications for them in this craft. However, the sewn sculpture examples in this book were made with either a 1902 treadle machine or a 1962 electric with a simple zigzag stitch.

Shears

Treat yourself to one pair of seven-inch or eight-inch fabric shears of the best quality you can afford. They should be of sufficient weight to cut heavy materials easily, and light enough that they won't tire you. A second pair of shears will be useful for cutting threads, patterns, and trimmings. Pinking shears are useful for cutting fabric that frays readily. For hand sewing, a small pair of manicure scissors with curved blades will be useful in many instances where straight scissors will not.

Needles

In addition to the usual sewing-machine needles, you may need ball-point needles for knit fabrics and triangular-point needles for leather and leatherlike materials.

Your collection of hand-sewing needles should *someday* include curved upholstery needles, a sailmaker's needle, a carpet needle, embroidery needles, tapestry needles, and glover's needles (for leather). A needle threader is useful for threading the sewing-machine needle with heavy threads, and when threading a glover's needle with waxed thread for leatherwork.

Although I don't usually wear a thimble, I have had use for a sailmaker's palm thimble on leather projects, and I find a simple leather thimble very comfortable. When you are stitching with very bulky thread for long periods of time, a two-inch-wide leather band worn around the first joint of the index finger (sewing hand) helps in gripping the needle.

Pressing Aids

An iron and portable sleeve board at your work table is sufficient for most sewn sculpture seam pressing. A pressing mitt, a tailor's ham, or even an oven mitt is useful for pressing small curved seams. A point presser is a small, flat wooden tool, handy for turning and pressing pointed shapes.

Stuffing Aids

Wood dowels, ¼-inch to ½-inch diameter, are useful for packing stuffing into small areas where fingers won't reach. A rubber band wrapped tightly around the tamping end of the dowel gives the traction needed to carry the stuffing along.

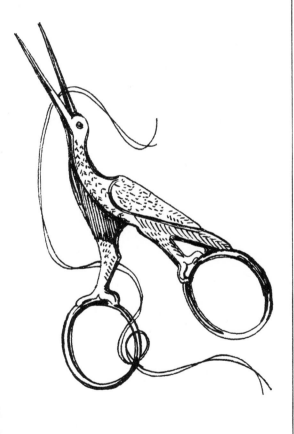

Design: The Key to Aesthetic Durability

"THERE is no such thing as bad design; there is only design or the lack of it." — *William Moore*

Design is the means of creating visual order within a piece of artwork. It is essential to all arts and crafts. This condensation of a basic design course is specifically related to the craft of sewn sculpture, but all design thinking can be traced to the rudimentary concepts.

Idea and Concept — the Prerequisites of Design

As you look at the sewn sculpture in this book, deciding which piece to make, you are responding to your perceptions of the objects and evaluating them with regard to their possible use or audience in your world. The moment you decide what to make, you have the first element of a successful piece — an idea.

The toad pictured on page 46 was created for my daughter, Maggie, aged four and in her toad period at the time. The idea grew from these observations: like many toddlers, Maggie likes real toads; she would like a toad to hold and to play with, and to take to bed at night; she would like, in effect, a teddy-bear toad — a soft, predictable, sympathetic toad.

To avoid making a meaningless (trite or outlandish) piece, you must establish a concept — a clarification of your idea. A concept is very simply established by the honest evaluation of the subject matter (your idea), the audience, and the medium, each in relationship to the others. If you are truly objective in your evaluations, you will always come up with a unique concept and probably a unique piece — because the relationships among subject matter, audience, and medium, and your relationship to them all, are unique. Therein lies the basis for a successful piece of art.

Let us conceptualize the idea, a cloth toad for Maggie. The subject matter is a toad, the audience is Maggie, and the medium is sewn sculpture. A real toad, an American toad (best known to Maggie), has these qualities: it is large among toads; it has moist-feeling skin, smooth sides and belly, rough back and head; it has sharp claws; its body feels squashy and soft on the underside, firm on top; it has shiny black, round eyes, wide-set and protruding; it is mottled beige and browns, dark on top, lighter underneath; it has a relatively large mouth. An American toad burrows in dirt and mud, leaps, remains motionless for hours, croaks, eats insects, and swims. Through the medium of soft sculpture, I can easily represent those toad qualities which Maggie finds fascinating and, in addition, those qualities which would make a toad *more* delightful to her.

Maggie's cloth toad might be of the colors she likes best, and in materials that will take the abuse of play. It should be small enough for her to hold easily, but a giant among real toads — perhaps a prince. (Maggie refers to toads as "he's.") The stuffing might provide a smooth, squashy feeling on the underside; a firmer, bumpy top side; and a sense of real weight. Foam rubber stuffing might even give a wiggly sensation — Maggie would like that. This toad might have firm, skinny legs to dangle when he's lifted, as if he were leaping. His forms and gesture should resemble a pose typical of real toads, but his expression might mirror Maggie's occasional drollery (which *I* find delightful).

This toad need not be just another stuffed toad. It can be unique, conveying my specific perceptions of Maggie, of toads, and of sewn sculpture.

American Toad conveys a fascination with the textural pattern of the subject through the medium of etching. An entirely different concept of a similar subject resulted in the tin frog, a toy designed for a general audience.

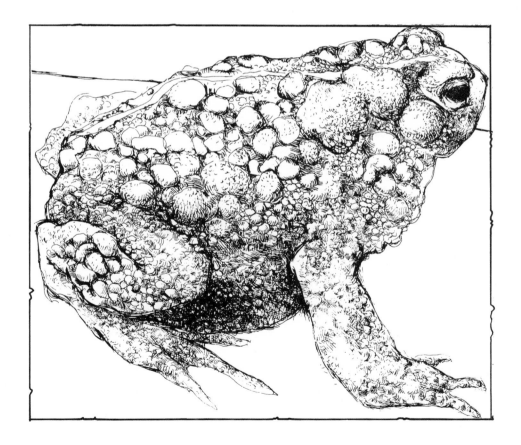

It characterizes frogs in general, by means of its jumping mechanism, shape, and surface graphics.

Conceptualizing helps narrow the infinite artistic possibilities within any subject matter to one specific possibility that you, the artist, can describe with clarity through the various qualities of your medium. In sewn sculpture three-dimensional form, shape, gesture, line, color, pattern, and texture are the means of expression.

You are designing the moment you consider any surface or form for the expression of concept. Earlier (page 22), we discussed the use of forms and surface qualities for their symbolic value to a concept. Now, by becoming aware of the purely visual and tactile relationships between elements, it will be possible for you to control not only the symbolism but also the aesthetics of the work as a whole.

Design is the logical selection and arrangement of elements for order and interest.

The Surface Design Elements of Sewn Sculpture
Although you will probably make your first sewn sculpture pieces from already designed patterns, your perceptions of a piece, as well as your concept

and, therefore, your emphasis, will influence the finished appearance of that piece. The size you choose to work in and even your perceptions of the individual shapes you cut, sew, and stuff will alter the forms and gesture of your piece to some degree. But, most noticeably, the surface qualities of the materials you select are the first elements with which you will be designing. So let us bypass the designing of three-dimensional forms for now and evaluate, instead, the surface elements of sewn sculpture.

Color

An understanding of the visual effects of color combinations based on their position in the color wheel will help you analyze your color choices and your reactions to color statements in your own or someone else's work. The color wheel (page 18) is an excellent analytical instrument; but the myriad colors of fabrics are far more exciting than painted, photographed, and printed colors. The color wheel is based on the colors of the spectrum — white light diffracted and arranged by a prism into bands of colored light, with invisible infrared to red at one end and violet to invisible ultraviolet at the other. In the translation of the colors of the spectrum to the color wheel, the two ends are joined. The colors of the color wheel are red, orange, yellow, green, blue, and violet.

In dyes and other coloring agents, the primary colors are red, yellow, and blue — the colors from which all other colors are made. The three secondary colors result from combinations of any two primary colors: orange, from red and yellow; green, from blue and yellow; violet, from blue and red. By combining neighboring primary and secondary colors on the color wheel, new colors are made: red-orange, yellow-orange, yellow-green, blue-green, blue-violet, and red-violet.

The visual aspects of color include hue (the color itself), value (its dark/light quality), and intensity (its degree of brightness or purity). In addition, colors are often referred to as being warm or cool. Blue and colors containing blue (green, yellow-green, blue-green, blue-violet, violet) are usually considered cool colors. Yellow, red, and red-related colors (red-violet, red-orange, orange, yellow-orange) are considered warm colors. As a rule, cool colors appear to recede; warm colors appear to advance. Intense colors and light values usually appear to advance, while grayed colors and dark values usually appear to recede. A grayed color is one that has been dulled by either the opposing color on the color wheel or black.

Pattern and Texture

Pattern, either printed, appliquéd, embroidered, or textural, can be utilized to control the appearance of forms. Pattern may be static or directional, visually active or calm, large or small (relative to the form on which it appears). For example, a pattern of stripes or arrows is directional; an all-over pattern of dots or checks is static. A rambling pattern of swirls and varying shapes in bright colors is visually active; one of grayed colors with more evenly distributed shapes of less variation is a more calm pattern. Pattern can exaggerate a form, distort it, or visually obscure it.

The surface texture of an object is usually seen before it is touched; so textural pattern (such as bumps, ridges, waffle pattern) or smoothness is visual as well as tactile and is read as dots, stripes, checks, or plain surface. Rough-textured, very bulky, and long-pile fabrics, like very large or active printed patterns, may obscure any but the most broad gesture and the simplest form, unless the sculpture in which they are used is very large.

Fabric absorbs or reflects light depending not only upon its color qualities but also upon its surface or textural quality. A lustrous surface reflects light; a dull or matte surface absorbs light. Pile fabrics, such as velvet, both reflect and absorb light, depending upon the direction in which the pile is brushed. A lustrous surface gives the illusion of greater size than it has in reality. Areas of dull surfaces appear smaller than they are.

The Primary Element of Order: A Design Theme

In making a piece from an existing pattern, the first element you select will probably be a fabric. Its qualities should help clarify and elaborate upon the concept. The second element you choose, combined with the first, begins to establish a design theme in the finished piece and should also enhance the concept. Every selection thereafter should further enhance the concept *and* support the design theme. A design theme, the primary element of order in a piece, may be one of comparison or contrast between design elements (color, texture, pattern, or shape), or of variations or repetition of one or more of the design elements.

Contrast and Comparison

Design is relationships. Very close relationships are referred to as comparisons, while very distant relationships between elements are referred to as contrasts. As a general rule, contrast produces excitement; comparison produces tranquillity or calm. For example, the use of blue and orange together creates more visual excitement than the use of yellow and orange. Blue and orange are directly opposite one another on the color wheel and are related only by the fact that they are both colors. Yellow and orange are closely related colors, orange being made up of red and yellow. Yellow and orange create a color comparison.

Yellow and violet are opposite colors and therefore contrasting colors. Dark and light are opposites and therefore contrasting values. Flowers and stripes are contrasting patterns, for the shapes with which they are made are circles and rectangles — contrasting shapes. Spheres and cubes are contrasting forms. Large and small are contrasting amounts. Rough and smooth contrast texturally.

Transitions may be created in a number of ways between any two opposing elements or qualities. Any element reminiscent of both opposites is a transitional element. For example, red is opposite green on the color wheel, and yellow-orange is midway between them. Yellow-orange has some of the characteristics of both red and green. Yellow-orange is literally a transition between red and green. Wavy lines might act as a transition between flowers and stripes. Ovals or arches might be transitions between circles and rectangles. A medium value is a transition between dark and light.

One method of creating transitions between opposing surface elements is through the use of printed patterns, appliqué, or embroidery. For example, by adding a spot of red to a green area and vice versa, or by adding a third area containing a green and red print, a transition is made between red and green. A transitional element between a sphere and a rectangle might be a printed pattern made up of rounded and straight shapes and used on either or both forms or on a third form, which, if a cylinder, becomes a transitional element in itself.

Variation and Repetition

Variation of one shape, color, pattern, or texture might be employed to give visual order to your work while embellishing a concept. The toad, for example, might be round, with spherical bumps and eyes and disc-shaped toes, and in fabrics with printed dots and rings. The design theme is variations of a shape (a circle).

Repetition of any single element may also be the design theme of a sewn sculpture, with the drama or excitement heightened by an accent of some contrasting element.

The Elements of Drama

Varying degrees of dramatic interest are achieved through the proportions in which the design elements are used, the manner in which they are arranged, and, finally, by the staging of the finished sculpture.

Proportion

The worst thing that can happen is to end up with equal emphasis on any two or more design elements, or themes. Proportion is probably the most important single design consideration in making any piece of artwork. In each group of elements utilized, one element must be dominant; all other elements must be subordinate. The greater the dominance of one element, the more dramatic will be the effect, or the more successful the piece. As the designer, you will decide how dominant is dominant as you determine the proportions of each element.

A good rule for establishing excitement through proportions is 70 per-

44

cent for the dominant element, 25 percent for one subordinate element, 5 percent for another subordinate element or "accent" element — or, more generally, large, medium, and small. This rule may be applied to each of the elements. With regard to color, for example, the rule means large, medium, and small amounts of the various colors used; bright, medium, and grayed intensities; dark, medium, and light values.

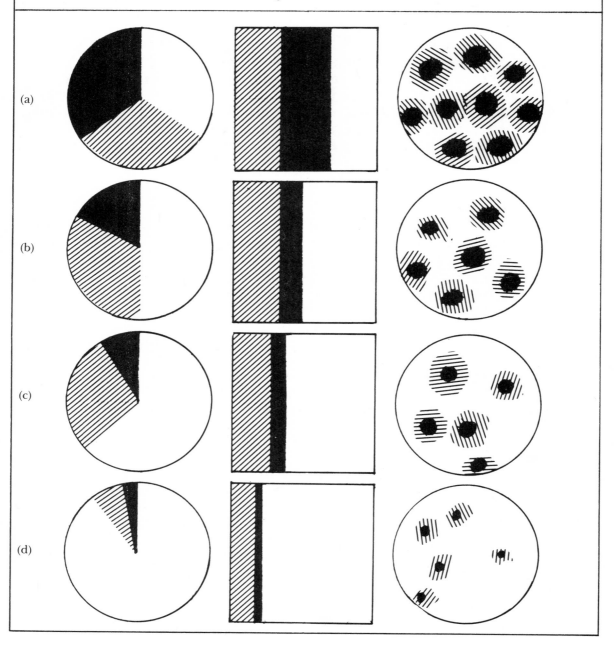

(a)

(b)

(c)

(d)

If you select orange as the dominant color, the subordinate colors might be yellow-orange and red-orange, establishing a theme of comparisons. If you use these colors in nearly the same amounts, intensities, and values, the piece will be boring. If you make about 70 percent of the piece bright, light orange, about 25 percent grayed, medium yellow-orange, and 5 percent bright, dark red-orange, your piece will sparkle even though your colors are closely related.

If you choose red as the dominant color, and green and yellow-orange as the subordinate colors, you are establishing a design theme of contrasting color. If your piece is 70 percent bright, medium-value red, 25 percent grayed, light yellow-orange, and 5 percent intense, dark green, the contrast is heightened by intensities and values, and emphasized even more by proportion. The piece will be *very* exciting — it'll rattle your eyes!

Diagrams (a-d) illustrate the degree of visual excitement created by various proportions of light, medium, and dark values from the least dramatic, or static (a), to the most dramatic (d).

This rule of proportion, or dominance of one element or statement, applies to each area (form or shape) of a three-dimensional design. For example, if shape is to be the dominant statement, do not confuse this dominance by making the shape (or three-dimensional form) from a wildly patterned or textured fabric that obscures or visually destroys the shape (or form).

Composition

The distribution of dominant and subordinate elements throughout a design (flat or three-dimensional) is, in effect, the viewing guide. We have discussed the fact that bright, warm colors appear to advance, and dark, cool colors appear to recede (page 41); and how visual excitement is created by greater contrasts (page 42). These visually active effects may become the means by which you gain some degree of control over the viewing pattern your audience follows when "reading" your sewn statements.

We read from left to right in the Western world, and unless some visual stimulation guides our eyes in some other pattern, we tend to read art and everything else in the same way. For example, if the toad is facing to the right (page 46), you probably will quickly scan the body left to right to focus on the most visually active area, which calls your attention from the perimeter of your natural range of vision. Since you read from left to right, the dominant but visually unstimulating shape of the toad's back guides you into the valley of the neck without interruption, where the activity created by the shiny eye bead draws your focus; and the dome shape of the eye socket and activity of folds creating the eyelid hold your interest awhile. If the toad is facing left, you will naturally focus on its visually active eye area first.

By the same general rule, any visually active area in any one view of a

sewn sculpture will attract the eye. By utilizing the dominant-subordinate rule, one visually active area will be more so than any of the others; in this way, some control is gained over which area is viewed first.

Directional devices such as triangular shapes and forms, arrowlike folds of pleats and gathers, and patterns, textures, or stitches that suggest a direction are all useful to the designer as a means of guiding attention from one area or element to another all around the piece.

Setting and Audience, or Staging

Setting — where and with what the finished piece is to be placed or most often seen — should be considered as a part of the design. The shape, color, texture, pattern, and symbolic connotations of the setting become, in effect, an extension of the sculptural piece. The same rules of contrast and comparison, proportion, and consideration of composition may be applied to the object's visual or symbolic relationship to the setting. For example, a comparison between a vertical piece of soft sculpture and a three-dimensional corner in which it is placed is less exciting than the same vertical sculptural piece contrasted with a dominantly horizontal flat wall. Another example might be found by placing a puffy pillow on a puffy sofa, creating such a close comparison of forms that the pillow is hardly noticeable — which may well be exactly the effect desired. If a more dramatic form statement is desired, the puffy pillow should be placed on a severe bench.

The elephant steps on a tiny box, and becomes gigantic.

An example of the relationship between the sculptural object and its audience is illustrated on page 89, where a great contrast in size between the object, a large bear, and the audience, a small boy, creates visual excitement.

The character of a piece of sewn sculpture seems to change with the setting. For example, if an object-pillow is placed on a sofa, it may be seen as just another clever pillow. Place that same object-pillow on a pedestal and it becomes art. *The unexpected is always exciting.*

Granny (page 87) in the nursery is a huge doll and a lap for the cat and child to sit on. In a museum (page 48), she is a piece of art. In a store window she is a prop, a symbolic decoration. In the spare room, upstairs, she is macabre — perhaps too emotionally stimulating for most audiences.

Learning Design Through Practice

There is no better way — in fact, there is no *other* way — to assimilate these basic elements of design than by working with them. If you'd like to try out some design thinking through exercises, as you would do in a basic three-dimensional design course, make a number of some small item such as the toad (page 92), each with a different concept and design theme. You will quickly discover the visual richness and excitement you can create by bringing these elements together in your own work; your sculptural pieces will be more meaningful.

Working with the Medium

AKING SOFT SCULPTURE differs from dressmaking in only minor respects. Since the fabric forms will be stuffed rather than draped over a figure, lengthwise and crosswise grains generally may be used interchangeably. Most seams do not require pressing, and there are no linings, facings, interfacings, or the dreaded buttonholes of tailoring. A basic knowledge of machine and hand-sewing techniques is enough to see you through all the projects in this book.

Pattern Preparation

Nearly all the patterns here have been greatly reduced to fit the pages and must be enlarged to their original sizes to make sculpture pieces like the examples shown.

With pencil and a ruler, lightly draw a grid over the pattern page (or on tracing paper laid over the page). Use the tick marks around the page as a guide for your grid lines. If the pattern scale is 1 square equals 2 inches, draw a grid (with the same number of squares), on large paper, with each square measuring 2 inches.

Copy the pattern shapes, square by square, on the large grid. Include construction marks and the grain-direction lines.

Enlarge or reduce the patterns by increasing or decreasing the inch equivalents shown on the pattern page.

Caution: Since you will be drawing the scaled pattern pieces free-hand, be especially careful that enlarged pattern pieces are the proper dimensions. To do this, pin enlarged pattern pieces together according to instructions. Make adjustments if necessary. When they align properly, remove pins, lay flat on material, and cut.

General Procedure with Woven Fabrics

Choosing Fabrics

As you select materials for your sculpture, consider the scale of the fabric texture, weight, and print in relation to the size of the object. Consider the surface qualities, as well as the material's flexibility, durability, and bulk. Does it have enough body to hold the large shapes and not too much body to conform to the details of the pattern design? Consider the symbolic use you will be making of the material. Will the material enhance or conflict with your idea? By keeping your concept foremost in your mind, you will easily answer the questions in this checklist.

Fabric Preparation

Prewash the fabric *only* if the finished sculpture will require washing. The sizing in new material is often an advantage during cutting and assembly of the sculpture piece.

Lay out the fabric and pattern pieces with consideration for nap, grain (straight or bias), and the number of pieces to be cut from each pattern shape. Pin the pattern, cut the fabric, and mark construction details on the fabric pieces as usual.

Assembly

Pin or baste the pieces together (usually right sides together) in the order suggested in the instructions, watching for areas that are to be left unstitched for stuffing and those that are to be left open for the addition of finished, stuffed parts of the sculpture.

Stitching

Adjust the sewing machine tension for the fabric thickness and thread you are using.

Stitch as usual, unless the instructions suggest a particular type of seam. See "Types of Seams" (page 50).

Before turning a stitched piece right side out, clip

seam margins as follows: across corners (a), to reduce bulk; inward toward seam line around curves (b), to avoid tension in outward curves and bunching in inward curves; toward apex of V shapes (c); and in varying widths (d), to reduce bulk where there are several layers.

Stuffing
Turn the stitched pieces right side out, using a point presser for sharp corners and a thin dowel for "finger" shapes.

Stuff the shapes "with feeling," or with regard for the character of the soft form you are creating. A dowel is useful for packing the filler into small shapes.

Close the stuffed piece with one of the hand-stitching methods below.

Types of Seams
The seam is the linear statement, as well as the structural foundation of sewn sculpture. The following types of seams are suggested for various pieces in this book:

Simple Seam (e), Lapped Seam (f), Butt Seam (g), Flat Felled Seam (h). The last is the strongest type of seam. A simple seam is stitched first on the right side of the fabric; one seam margin is trimmed away, and the second seam margin is lapped over the first and top-stitched.

Hand Stitching
Many decorative stitches may be borrowed from embroidery for seams and for ornamenting sculptural pieces. The following hand-stitching methods are suggested as seam closures for projects in this book.

RUNNING STITCH (i): used to join pieces quickly and temporarily (basting) and to make gathers.

DOUBLE NEEDLE STITCH (j): Running Stitch worked with two needles in opposition. Most often used in leatherwork, it resembles the straight stitch made by a sewing machine.

COBBLER'S STITCH (k): Running Stitch worked first in one direction, then in the other. It is an

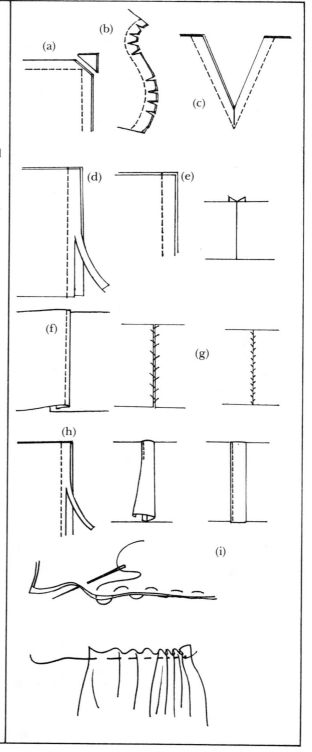

alternative to Double Needle Stitch and Back Stitch. It is often used in leatherwork.

BACK STITCH (1): a long stitch underneath, a short stitch on top. It resembles a straight machine stitch on the top side.

WHIP STITCH OR OVERCAST STITCH (m): used where a raised seam is desired, or as a simple catch stitch for joining two pieces.

BLIND HEM STITCH (n): a hidden stitch used for joining two stuffed pieces.

FISHBONE STITCH (o): an ornamental stitch used to close a butt seam in heavy materials. This was probably man's first stitch.

Special Considerations for Leather

There are lovely subtleties in leatherwork that you will discover from your own experience, and from that of leather craftsmen who share their findings through books. Only those rudiments of sewing with leather which are directly related to the leather examples in this book are mentioned here.

Pattern Preparation

Make complete patterns rather than half patterns with fold-line edges. Leather is never folded for cutting.

Arrange the pattern pieces on either the grain side or the flesh side of the leather, avoiding undesirable imperfections and weak areas. Consider the degree of stretch required by each pattern piece. Turn the patterns over to cut identical but opposing shapes.

Weight the pattern pieces or secure them to the leather with masking tape. Use a stylus, an awl, or a tracing wheel to trace the cutting lines on the grain side, a ball point pen or wax chalk on the flesh side.

Cutting

It is usually possible to cut garment weight (1- to 3-ounce) leather with dressmaker's shears. A sharp craft knife or single-edge razor blade will cut all weights of leather.

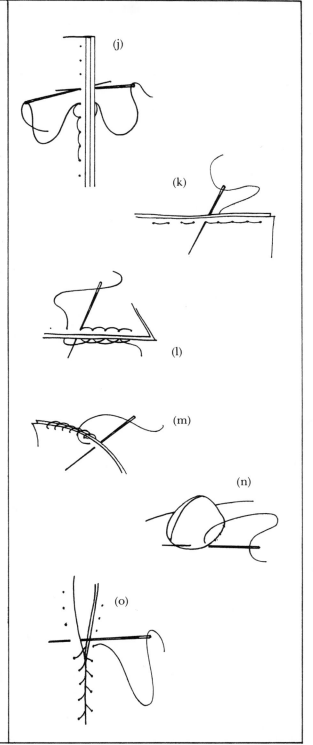

Cut fur and fleece as suggested for long-pile fabrics, page 53.

To reduce bulk in seams, the edges of the leather pieces may be skived or thinned with a safety beveler or other skiving tool.

Special Forming, or Wet-Shaping
Leather may be molded to create three-dimensional forms without the aid of seams. Thoroughly soak the leather in warm water. Stretch it over a hard form, tacking the edges with small nails as you pull the leather taut (p). Allow it to dry slowly, away from heat. Remove the nails and the mold, and trim the leather to the desired shape.

Assembly
Rubber cement may be used in the seam margins to temporarily join leather pieces that are to be stitched. Alternatives are paper clips or masking tape.

Stitching
Leather of 1- to 3-ounce weight may be stitched on most home sewing machines, using a triangular-point needle. A roller presser foot, available for some machines, prevents the presser foot from sticking to the leather. Tissue paper stitched along with the seam accomplishes the same thing. The tissue is torn away afterward. Tissue under the leather prevents the leather from sticking to the machine surface.

Glues may be preferred in place of stitching in some areas. Two reliable leather adhesives are Sobo glue and Barge cement, Sobo being the easier to use.

Use triangular-point glover's needles for hand stitching, except when stitching holes are prepunched; then use a tapestry needle.

An edge creaser tool is generally used to indent stitching lines evenly along the edges.

A spacing wheel rolled along the stitching lines makes indentations at regular intervals for stitching holes. A #6 spacing wheel makes six marks per inch.

(p)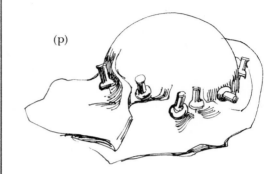

An awl is commonly used to make small holes for stitching with waxed linen or similar thread. Place three or four thicknesses of corrugated cardboard under the leather to punch the holes.

Since leather is a non-fraying material, the simplest seams are used in leatherwork. Work for even tension in your hand stitching to avoid puckers.

See "Types of Seams" and "Hand Stitching" (page 50).

Seams in leather are generally more beautiful if they are evened out and slightly flattened by tapping them with a rawhide mallet. A good substitute is a wood mallet or a hammer, covered with a leather scrap.

Special Considerations for Long-Pile Fabrics (Fake Fur)

Bulk, direction, and length of the pile are the only aspects of fake fur that require special consideration.

Pattern Preparation

Make complete patterns rather than half patterns with fold-line edges. Long-pile fabrics are never folded double for cutting.

Place the pattern pieces on the back of a single thickness of fabric, noting the direction of the pile, and allowing space to turn the pieces over to cut identical, but opposing shapes.

Cutting

Slide the point of the shears under the backing fabric and between the long fibers to avoid chopping the pile (q).

To eliminate bulk, shear the pile from the seam margins of each fabric piece, using an electric hair clipper or fabric shears (r).

Assembly

Use ball-head pins to join the pieces. Ball-head pins set crosswise in the seam margins are more easily seen and handled than regular pins.

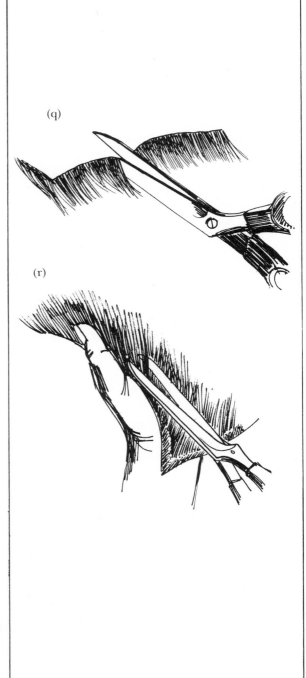

(q)

(r)

Stitching

Use a #14 sewing-machine needle and nylon or polyester thread. Back-stitch all seams at the start and end. Seams in fake fur are very difficult to mend after a piece is stuffed.

Turn the stitched pieces right side out and, using a fork, rake the seams to release the pile fibers that are caught. This hides the seams.

Special Considerations for Knits

The direction and degree of stretch in knit fabrics are the only aspects which require special mention here.

Use nylon or polyester thread for seams that will "give" a little. To eliminate bunching while securing the thread at the start of a seam, begin stitching about ¼ inch inside the starting edge, and back-stitch to that edge.

As you stitch forward, gently stretch the fabric, holding it in front of and behind the presser foot. Your pull should not hamper the fabric feed of the machine. A trial run with a scrap of the fabric will help you determine the amount of stretch necessary to create the desired "give" in the seam.

To make nonstretch seams, which will be indented in the stuffed piece, stitch the seams onto a narrow strip of woven fabric or twill tape, and do not stretch the fabric as you stitch.

Surface Ornamentation

All forms of ornamentation suitable for fabric and related materials are certainly applicable to sewn sculpture pieces; and since your own stitchery, printing, or dyeing may be designed to support a specific sculptural theme, it may be more effective than commercially printed surfaces.

The advancing and receding aspects of color and texture mentioned on pages 41–42 may become as important as seams and darts for manipulating form. By the use of acrylics, dyes, inks, and so on, graphic shading may be applied to a fabric form, to give the illusion of form where little exists, or to emphasize form, as with the rough Head examples (page 128), and the silk-screened Rabbit (page 25).

The Barn Owl (page 56) utilizes needlepoint to add a sense of naturalistic coloring to the subject matter and to help emphasize the sculptural forms through subtle shading. A batiked pattern enriches the leather Gentlebeast (pages 56, 127) with a dappled effect.

There are many good books dealing with stitching techniques, fabric printing, and batik and other dye methods. A few titles are listed on page 35.

All of these techniques, as well as burning (with an electric stylus), are applicable to leather. Beadwork and embroidery are age-old forms of decorating leather pieces. In addition, tooling and numerous lacing patterns found in Mexican and Spanish leather articles are worth investigating for use in sewn sculpture.

Batik, in which wax is used to resist dye, is the one less common form of surface decoration utilized in this book. Directions follow for your convenience.

A Simple Batik Method for Fabric
Choose a fabric made of primarily natural fibers for the best dyeing results.

If you feel insecure at the thought of waxing the material freehand, you may lightly outline the proposed wax areas with an artist's charcoal stick. Place the fabric on waxed paper or in a large embroidery hoop to facilitate wax penetration into the fabric.

Melt special batik wax (usually about 4 ounces is sufficient), or one part beeswax and one part paraffin, in a *heavy* pan, preferably with a cooking thermometer attached to, but not touching, the side. If you don't have a heavy pan, melt the wax in a tin can in a saucepan with an inch or so of boiling water. A clothespin will secure the can to the side of the pan. Bring the wax mixture to somewhere between 120 and 140°F; the wax will be smoking slightly. The wax cools quickly and therefore must be applied quickly, frequently dipping the brush or other applicator into the hot wax. The wax must penetrate the cloth in order to resist the dye properly. If necessary, wax both sides.

Use special batik dye or regular fabric dye. Mix the dye powder with salt and a little warm water to the consistency of thin paste. Add the dye solution and a little household soda to warm, not hot, water in a plastic basin. Make a very strong dye solution. Test the dye color and value on a scrap of the fabric you intend to use.

Submerge the waxed fabric in the warm dye bath and allow it to soak, stirring it occasionally, until the color is a shade darker than the value desired. For a crackled effect, wad the fabric to crack the wax, enabling the dye to seep into the fabric through the cracks.

The batik design suggested for the Marble Cone shell pillow (page 69) requires only minimal brush waxing, a mere introduction to batik. You may enjoy using a traditional batik tool called a tjanting, a small copper cup with a fine spout, mounted on a wooden handle, for line work. Repeated waxing and dyeing is required for a multicolored design, and there the excitement of batik begins. If you wish to investigate the craft, you will find one of the batik books listed on page 35 helpful.

Remove the wax by ironing the batiked fabric between sheets of plain newsprint paper with a medium-hot iron, replacing the wax-saturated paper frequently until all the wax is removed. Cleaning solvent (white spirit solvent) will remove the last traces of wax from the fabric and from the brush. To clean the pan, scrape out as much of the hardened wax as possible. Reheat the pan enough to melt the remaining wax and wipe it away with newspaper. Wash the pan in detergent.

Leather Batiking

Batik leather pieces while they are flat, or after they are stitched together and lightly stuffed if you wish to follow the forms of the sculpture with your batik designs. Leather that has been preshaped may also be batiked.

Melt the wax mixture and apply as for fabric batik, brushing the hot wax onto the leather with quick, sure strokes, or using a tjanting for more uniform linear patterns. Practice on scraps to gain confidence with the tjanting or brush. To obtain a crackled effect, wad or pinch the waxed leather to wrinkle it just as you would with fabric. The dye will seep into the cracks.

Wearing plastic gloves, use a soft brush or wool dauber to apply leather dye evenly to the entire surface or only to the areas you wish dyed. Allow the dye to penetrate and to dry completely.

To remove the wax, place clean newsprint paper over the waxed leather and iron over the paper with a medium-hot iron. Quickly replace the wax-saturated paper with clean paper until all the wax is removed.

To remove wax from pieces that have been preshaped but not yet stitched, hold the piece with an oven mitt to retain the shape of the leather while ironing out the wax. Some reshaping will be necessary after the batiking and wax removal. The leather will respond quickly without soaking.

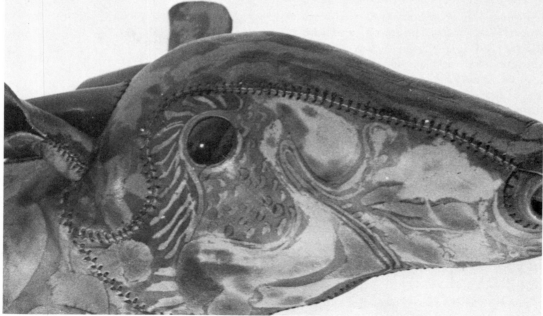

Developing Skills and Confidence in the Only Way Possible — by Producing

As you work from the patterns in this book, you will be choosing your materials to enhance your own concepts based on the subject matter, the intended audience, and use of the finished sculpture. By these choices you may completely change the finished appearance, mood or attitude, and/or connotations of the piece. You may decide to make changes in the pattern shapes themselves, or in sizes only; or you may use the designs just as they are shown in order to gain a little experience before venturing further into this medium.

Each piece of sculpture here is nearly as easy to produce as any other, taken one step at a time — the way all things are made. If you are inspired by what appears to be a difficult piece I encourage you to purchase your materials, even if they are costly, and go to work. Your enthusiasm, along with the commitment in the form of materials, will see you through the most mind-boggling segments of the piece. Your energies will be well spent on a piece that excites you; its completion will give you a bonus of confidence for pieces to come.

Copying is the most expedient way to discover the intricacies of a craft and to gain confidence. The patterns in this book are, in effect, teaching tools, and since you are your own teacher, I hope you will use them freely as points of departure into your own realms of self-expression.

Note: I understand that visual-minded people (most craftsmen), are not always avid direction followers, and that a written direction for a simple sewing act is usually more cumbersome than the act it describes. As you become accustomed to my manner of phrasing directions and see the work progressing in your hands, I hope you will approach the projects here with increasing confidence. Truly awkward stages are noted to reassure you that you are not in some private predicament.

The Simplest "Pillow" and Geometric Forms
I refer to the forms that result from two identical shapes joined around the edges as "pillow" forms. They are the simplest sewn sculpture forms and more versatile than one might expect from first impressions. The addition of a third shape joining the edges changes what was to be a "knife-edge" form to a "box" form — the basis for sculptural pieces.

These first basic forms, simply constructed from simple shapes, are shown on page 18 as tiny, herb-scented pillows, doll cushions, pincushions, and whatever you imagine they are. Each surface pattern has been chosen for its relationship to the size and shape of the form on which it appears, and to enhance the scent of herbs, to endure the intended use, or to exploit a color, textural, or shape theme.

The experience you gain by making these basic pillow and geometric forms, and seeing them at intermittent stages of their development, adds to your understanding of the craft. To realize, for example, that a fully stuffed square-cut pillow has four concave sides, four conical corners, and two convex sides, is to add those forms (concave, conical, and convex) to your sewn sculpture repertoire, which is finally just as important to you, the craftsman, as the piece you are making.

You will realize by seeing this and other shapes transformed in your hands that you are not making an outline shape; you are making a three-dimensional form that has several shapes, and you will begin to look for and to recognize that form in each pattern. This may seem academic, but haven't you always regarded a square cut pillow as a square after it is stuffed? Although we refer to it as "square," we should see it for all the shapes it is — none of which is square, in fact.

Follow this general procedure as you make the basic forms given here:

Cut out the shapes, pin, and stitch them (with right sides together) as directed for the particular form you are making. Clip the seam margins of curved seams and across corners (see page 49 if this puzzles you). Turn the stitched piece right side out, stuff it, and close the opening with hand stitching.

Knife-Edge Form (A)
Stitch around the edge seam line, beginning at the small dot and ending at the large dot, leaving an opening between the dots for stuffing (a).

Dart-Corner Form (B)
Stitch each of the four sides, breaking the thread at the inverted corners (a). Leave an opening between the dots for stuffing. Fold one side seam to the next, matching the notches in each inverted corner (b). Stitch the corner seams, across the side seams (c).

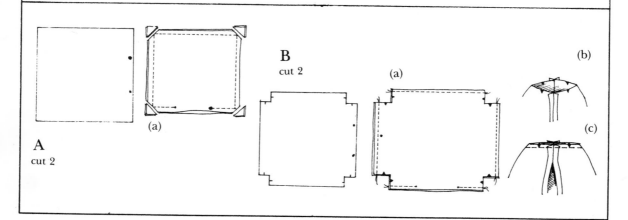

A
cut 2

(a)

B
cut 2

(a)

(b)

(c)

Box-Edge Form (C)
Fold the end seam margin of the edge strip to the wrong side of the fabric. Place the strip on one of the squares (right sides together), at the small dot, and align the seam lines of the strip and the squares (a). Stitch the strip to the square, stopping at each corner to raise the presser foot and turn the fabric to stitch the next edge (b). End by overlapping the starting edge (c). Reposition the fabric in order to stitch the two strip ends together. Stitch the edge strip to the second square in the same manner, leaving an opening in one side for turning the piece right side out and for stuffing (d).

Cone Form (D)
Join the two sides of the triangular shape, leaving an opening between the dots for turning (a). Add the circle (b), to the open base.

Gathered Tube Form (E)
Join the two ends of the rectangle, leaving an opening between the dots for turning and stuffing (a). Gather the top and bottom edges by hand or by machine, using heavy-duty thread. Pull the gathering stitches together, and wrap the gathered margin tightly with thread (b). Make a few stitches to secure the thread.

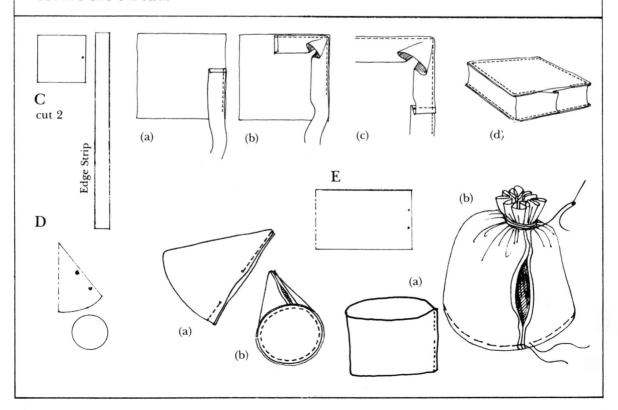

Opposing Squares Form (F)
Stack the two squares at opposing angles (a). Pin each corner to meet the corresponding side notch (b). Stitch the seam, leaving an opening for turning and stuffing (c).

Opposing Triangles Form (G)
Assemble as with the Opposing Squares.

Softball Form (H, I)
Place the two pieces at opposing angles, matching a large dot to a small dot (a). Pin the pieces together, matching large dots to small dots all around the joining edge, and stitch the seam, leaving an opening for turning and stuffing. This pattern produces a sphere when it is made up in a four-way stretch material (H) and a very different form in a woven fabric (I).

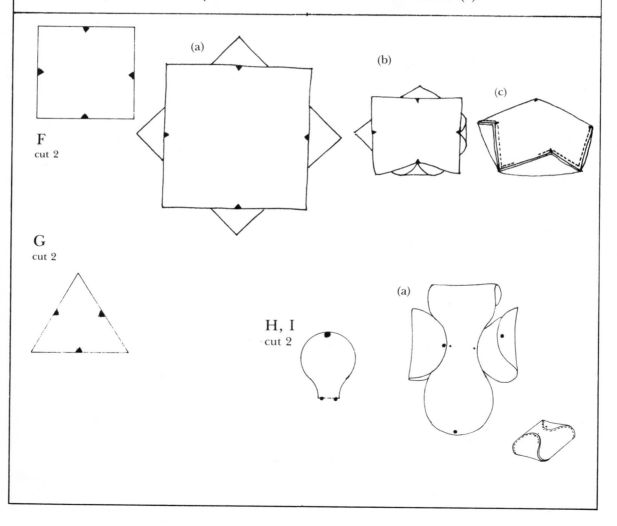

Spiral Form (J)

Do not cut out the shapes in fabric until the seam is stitched. Pin two pieces of fabric right sides together and lightly draw the pattern shape (seam line) on one of them (a). Stitch on the drawn line for a continuous seam, leaving an opening between the dots. Cut out the pieces, leaving narrow seam margins, and clip the margins at intervals (b). As you stuff this form, you will notice its tendency to turn inward, making a tighter spiral. The spiral can be manipulated to twist outward, like a ram's horn, or to curl more tightly inward, like a nautilus shell.

Closed Doughnut Form (K)

Lay out the fabric to cut one whole circle and one made up of two halves with the fabric selvages overlapping in the middle (a). Stitch the selvages, right sides together, leaving an opening at one end for turning and stuffing (b). Rejoin the two circles and stitch the edge seam all around. Clip the margins. Turn the piece right side out. Lightly draw the inner circle on the seamless side. Top-stitch (through both thicknesses) on the drawn line (c).

Globe Form (L)

Join the six elliptical shapes, leaving an opening between the dots in one seam for turning.

Try a spherical form made up of triangles (M), or of pentagons. Try a sewn and stuffed fantasy of your own design from a combination of forms from this group.

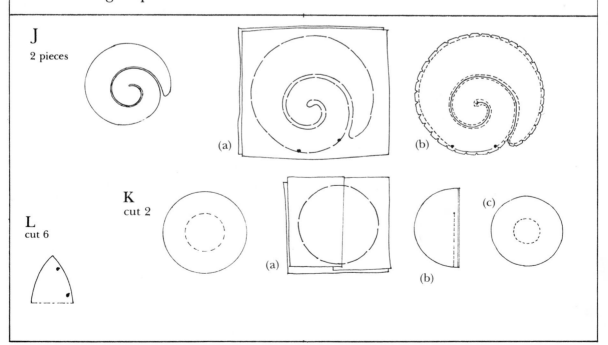

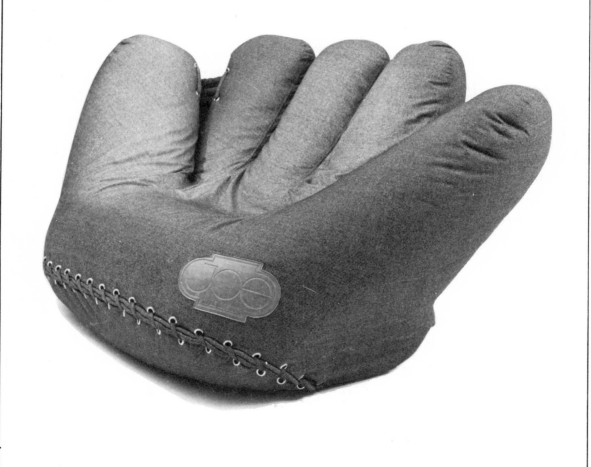

A Drastic Change in Size: Simple Furniture

BY A CHANGE in perception of the forms on page 18, pincushions become hassocks or chairs; herb pillows become floor cushions. The doughnut form or the great, showy spiral are just as likely to be lounge chairs. Two of the most obvious possibilities are the floor cushion and the Nest Chair pictured on pages 67 and 68.

The beanbag chair of the mid-sixties is a large spherical "skin," often a globe form, loosely stuffed with Styrofoam pellets — a furniture concept applicable to a number of geometric as well as asymmetric sewn forms. Large cushions, sewn, zippered, or belted together, or held by a simple wooden or metal frame, are common furniture concepts of our time. The Corbusier chair of the thirties is an example. The Play Pen by Selig is a huge sectional sofa or "soft environment" of the early seventies, and not unlike an oversized sofa designed by Jaromir Krejcar in the Art Deco period (the twenties and thirties). Perhaps you have seen Pop Art soft furniture such as the Stendig baseball mitt chair of the sixties, and less formidable folk pieces — stack cushions in the form of a hamburger, an upholstered chair with a head and hands, or a sewn cactus hat rack, to recall a few.

The transformation of unrelated forms into furniture is a natural outgrowth of our complete ease with the craft of sewing and with its unpretentious, comfortable materials.

Carpet and Cowhide Floor Cushion

EATHER WAS chosen for this piece (page 67) because of its great durability and its increasing beauty with use. The woven carpet is, of course, at home on the floor and provides a rich contrast to the smooth leather. The seams, hand-stitched with waxed linen thread, call attention to the design of the piece.

Any long-wearing upholstery material or cotton or linen canvas is suitable for this floor cushion. For less permanent, decorative cushions any relatively heavy fashion fabric will suffice. Other alternatives might include a patchwork quilt, a piece of needlepoint, fur, or hair sheepskin.

In large sewn and stuffed pieces, a combination of stuffing materials can provide bulk, firmness, and resilience without great weight. Foam rubber and polyester batting were used to fill this cushion and many of the larges pieces in this book.

Materials
3 sq. ft., or a 30'' – 34'' square of 4-oz. cowhide
A 31'' – 35'' square of carpet
Edge creaser or stylus and 36'' metal rule
#6 spacing wheel
Awl
#14 or #16 tapestry needle
Waxed linen thread
4 – 5 lbs. polyester fiber
2 foam rubber or polyurethane cushions, 22'' square, 4'' thick

Refer to page 51 if you have questions regarding the procedure for working with leather.

Directions
Follow the directions for assembling the Opposed Squares form on page 60, using one 34'' square of leather and one 35'' square of carpet.

1. Use steel rule, an edge creaser, and a spacing wheel to mark all 4 edges for stitching holes. Use an awl to make the stitching holes.

2. Cut the carpet piece with sharp shears, allowing at least 1'' margins all around.

3. Join the pieces as directed (page 60), securing them with safety pins. Working from the right side, stitch the seam by hand, with a tapestry needle and waxed linen thread. Fold the carpet margins to the inside as you work, stitching through two thicknesses of carpet. Either Running Stitch, Cobbler's Stitch, Double Needle Stitch, or Whip Stitch is suitable for this piece. (Refer to page 50 for stitch diagrams.)

4. When you have stitched 6 of the 8 edges around the cushion, insert the polyurethane or foam rubber pads at opposing angles, matching the square top and bottom surfaces of the cushion. Insert polyester fiber between the foam pads and around the edges.

5. Continue stitching to within about 10'' from the end. Add polyester fiber to fill the cushion. Finish the seam.

Nest Chair

GIANT PUFFED SLEEVE shape has been transformed into the chair pictured on page 68. The all-over floral and butterfly print in combination with the form suggests nestling in a garden. Polyester fiber around a foam rubber core provides softness and resilience, and cotton fabric adds to the comfort of this Nest Chair. The example, made for a teen-ager's room, is 28 inches high and 48 inches in diameter.

The form is adaptable to many moods through the use of leather, natural canvas, bright-colored or bold-print upholstery fabrics, velours, or fake furs. The piece may be permanently stitched, or strapped together for easy disassembly and washing.

Materials
5½ yds. 54''-wide heavy cotton fabric
#16 sewing-machine needle
Heavy-duty sewing-machine thread
Heavy-duty hand-sewing thread and needle
2 preformed polyurethane or foam rubber box cushions, each 18'' diam., 4 ins. thick
30 lbs. polyester fiber
Polyurethane or foam rubber padding (rolled), or 8''-diam. cylinders totaling 9' 4''

Additional Materials for a Leather-Strapped Version
4 belt strips, 8 – 10-oz. cowhide, each 1½'' wide, 6'' long
4 metal D-rings or 2 buckles for 1½''-wide belting
Edge creaser
Spacing wheel
Awl
3/16''-diam. leather punch (if buckle holes are needed)
#5 glover's needle and waxed linen thread
Sobo glue

Directions
Note: Follow steps 1, 2, 3, 5, 6, 10, and 14 only if the piece is to be strapped together. Refer to page 51 for special directions for working with leather.

(pattern appears on page 71)

1. Use the edge creaser to give a finished look to the grain-side edges of the leather straps, and to mark the stitching lines.

2. Using a spacing wheel, mark the lines for stitching holes as indicated by a dotted line on the pattern. Punch the holes with an awl.

3. Attach a buckle (a), or D-rings (b), to 2 straps. If a buckle is used, punch 3 or 4 holes in the second 2 straps with a leather punch.

4. Join center back seam D and Back and Side/Front chair pieces at seams A and B. For extra strength, make Flat Felled seams (page 50), but on the wrong side of the fabric for smoothness.

5. Position the Belt Facing strips on the wrong side of the fabric, as indicated on the pattern. Secure them with Sobo glue.

6. Place the leather straps in position on the right side of the fabric and stitch them to the chair fabric and facings with a glover's needle and waxed linen thread, using Cobbler's or Back Stitch (page 50).

7. Fold the chair fabric lengthwise (right sides together), to join, and stitch seam lines C, leaving the ends (to the triangles) unstitched.

8. Turn the piece right side out.

9. Working through the unstitched portion of seam C, join the two ends (right sides together), and stitch.

10. To finish the ends for a strapped chair, make long Running Stitches around each end (c). Gather the stitches to fit the circular End Pieces. Working through the unstitched portion of seam C, stitch the End Pieces to the gathered ends, right sides together (d).

11. Insert the stuffing materials through the unstitched portion of seam C, packing them densely.

12. Close seam C with hidden stitches (Blind Hem Stitch, page 51), using heavy-duty thread.

13. Refer to the directions on page 59 to make two round box-type cushions for the chair center.

14. Join the straps to form the chair tightly around the center cushions.

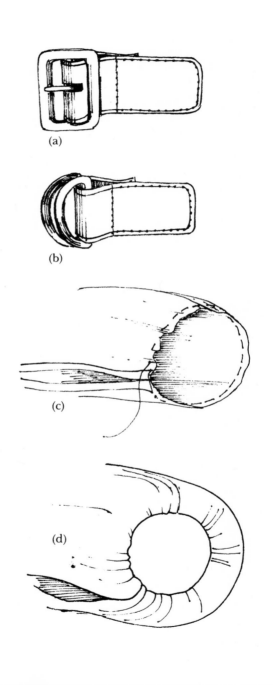

(a)

(b)

(c)

(d)

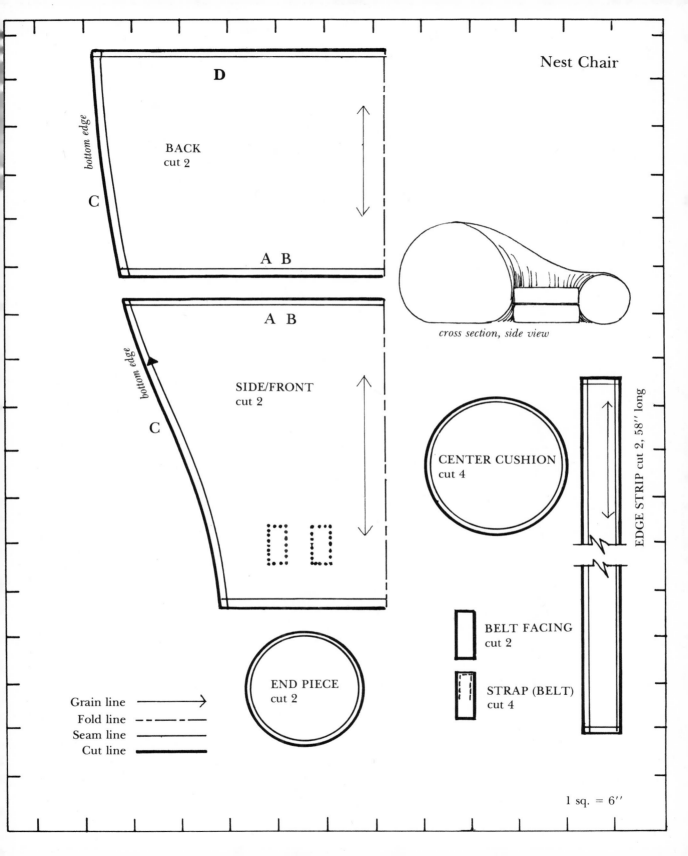

Nest Chair

D

BACK
cut 2

bottom edge

C

A B

cross section, side view

A B

bottom edge

SIDE/FRONT
cut 2

C

CENTER CUSHION
cut 4

EDGE STRIP cut 2, 58″ long

BELT FACING
cut 2

STRAP (BELT)
cut 4

END PIECE
cut 2

Grain line ⟶
Fold line ⟶
Seam line ⟶
Cut line ⟶

1 sq. = 6″

Pillow Forms Taken One Step Further: Object Pillows

OBJECT PILLOWS are the decorative results of a shift in emphasis from function to subject matter, or to a nonrepresentational design theme.

Noble Scallop and Marble Cone

THOUGH STILL USEFUL, the Noble Scallop and Marble Cone pillows pictured (page 69) are primarily decorative objects. They lack the humor present in Pop Art object pillows. They were not designed to emphasize the incongruity of soft shells but, rather, to bring a summer beach atmosphere indoors.

Many seashells are pillow-shaped, with surface qualities that quite naturally bring fabrics to mind, and vice versa. There are many pillow possibilities in this subject matter, and many different shell pillows may be made using these patterns as points of departure; perhaps with only the addition of needlework, or by the use of printed fabrics. Or the pillows might simply be made in more durable fabrics for the sun deck, the porch, or the beach.

The forms are retained by the use of foam rubber padding over a core of polyester batting. In the Noble Scallop the padding is machine-quilted to the outer fabric. Assembly by machine is awkward because of the bulk involved, but at least the shapes are simple.

Materials for Each Seashell Pillow
½''-thick polyurethane foam padding
3 lbs. polyester fiber
A yardstick and a pencil, or a tracing wheel and dressmaker's carbon
A few large safety pins
1 package tissue paper
Button and carpet thread
A sailmaker's needle
Dual-duty thread for machine stitching
Mercerized cotton thread for hand stitching

Special Directions
To make darts in foam padding, overlap the edges and stitch by hand with widely spaced Whip stitches.

When stitching foam on the sewing machine, use tissue above and below it to keep it from sticking to the presser foot and the machine surface. Tear the tissue to remove it from the finished seam.

Draw the quilting lines on the right side of the fabrics with a pencil, or trace them with a yardstick, tracing wheel, and dressmaker's carbon. The stitching and indentations will hide the lines.

(pattern appears on page 75)

Noble Scallop

Additional Materials
1 yd. 45''-wide pastel upholstery fabric

Directions

1. Cut 2 opposing fabric and foam pieces A. Trim the scalloped edge of the foam pieces to the seam line. Cut 2 fabric pieces B and one foam B. Trim edges 1, 2, 3 of the foam piece to the seam line.

2. Mark the quilting lines on both fabric pieces A and on one B.

3. Make darts separately in the foam and fabric pieces A.

4. Secure each fabric piece A right side up to the matching foam piece A with a few safety pins.

5. Using the largest straight machine stitch possible, sew the fabric piece A to the foam, following the quilting lines.

6. Pin the two fabric pieces B right sides together. Stitch three sides, leaving the side with dots unstitched. Turn the piece right side out.

7. Insert foam piece B. Using the largest machine straight stitch, stitch through all layers, following the quilting lines.

8. With right sides together, baste B to one scallop piece A, matching the large dots on B to the small dots at the apex and straight sides of A. B will be folded around the darted apex (a).

9. Pin the two pieces A with right sides together (B will be inside the scallop). Machine-stitch around the apex and one straight side of the scallop.

10. Remove the piece from the machine to hand-stitch the scalloped edge with Running Stitch. (The machine can be used, but it is more awkward.) Clip the seam margins on all curves and dips to prevent puckering.

11. Turn the piece right sides out, stuff, and close the straight side opening with hidden stitches (Blind Hem Stitch, page 51).

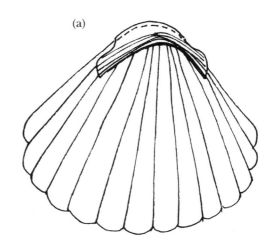

(a)

Marble Cone

Additional Materials
2/3 yd. each white and light-blue satin
Dark-brown fabric dye
Batik wax and supplies (page 54)

Directions

1. Cut one J of each: white and light-blue satin and foam. Trim foam J to the seam line at the S curve and on one side (between x's.) Cut one K of each foam and white satin.

2. Make darts separately in foam and fabric K pieces.

3. Batik dark-brown pattern on white satin J and K. (See the batik instructions, page 54.)

4. With right sides together, stitch the lower, S-curve edge of J between dots only. Clip the seam margins. Turn the piece right sides out.

5. Insert the foam piece (J) and pin all layers together. Stitch between arrows from the S-curve edge around. (One side of the shell is left open.) Trim the foam to the seam line from the S curve onward, between x's.

6. Curl the piece to make a cone shape, bringing the stitched side to the slash-dot line inside the curl. Curl the piece tightly at the point of the cone (b).

7. Folding the outside (batik print) layer of the unstitched end out of the way, hand-stitch through all other layers, following the slash-dot line. (Work from the outside of the foam.) This closes the shell into an open-top cone. (c).

8. Using hidden stitches, close the opening left in step 5.

9. Stuff the pillow to overflowing.

10. Mark the spiral quilting lines on the fabric K piece with pencil dots (pushing through the pattern at intervals), or with a tracing wheel and dressmaker's carbon paper.

11. Pin the fabric K to the foam piece, right side up. Use the longest straight machine stitch to quilt the pieces, following the spiral lines.

12. Pin the top (K) into position on the cone, tucking the margins inward. Stitch with hidden stitches to within 4″ of completion of the circle. Add stuffing, if necessary, to fill the pillow. Close the opening with hidden stitches.

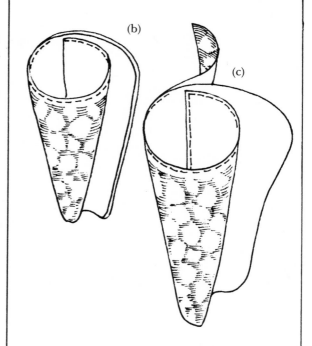

(b)

(c)

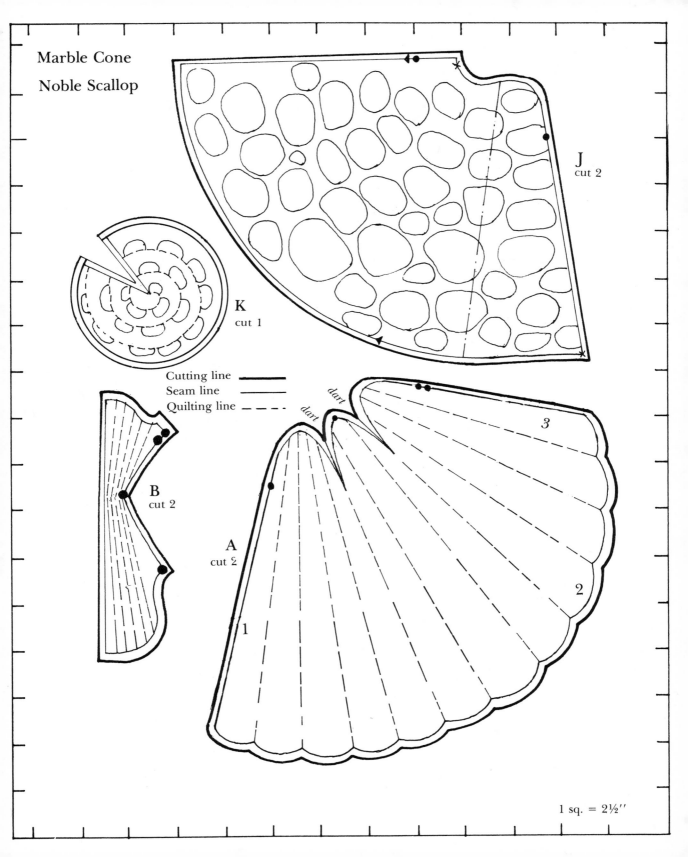

Marble Cone

Noble Scallop

J
cut 2

K
cut 1

Cutting line
Seam line
Quilting line

B
cut 2

A
cut 2

dart

dart

1

2

3

1 sq. = 2½''

Sewn Objects Designed for Play: Toys

FEW TOYS receive more abuse or more love from children than soft toys. An important part of the rehearsal for real-life roles, soft toys are whispered to, sung to, reasoned with in every conceivable tone, cried on, punched, squeezed, and kissed. They seem able to protect, to forgive, to scare people, and generally to become best friends.

It's impossible to know which soft toy will become a child's favorite, but since we usually transmit to our children some of our own early fascinations with the world, we can design toys with the details we remember from our favorites. We can choose subject matter, colors, and textures our children seem to like; and we can give each toy we make that very important quality character — the visual hint of a personality to get to know and to respond to, a personality that can seem to reflect the child's moods and support his or her fantasies.

If we are successful, if we choose the right subject for the moment and include elements of personal importance, our soft toy creations will someday look like dear old Trudy (below), who has even had stitches put in and removed with her child friend, and the All-American Toad, who at one point in its life with a boy had its foot bitten off.

Pillow Dolls

THE VERSATILE PILLOW DOLL is one step away from the dear old-fashioned sock doll. Lovably soft, and uncomplicated, it is an easy doll form to embellish with a few favorite prints, a little embroidery thread, two buttons, and a pair of small socks, if you wish.

Trudy has seen all the beds and toy baskets and playpens a doll is apt to see in six years and has been retired to the attic. She is made from polyester-cotton fabrics and has cotton knit socks for legs and hands.

The Sisters (below) were made by a twelve-year old girl in her first attempt at doll-making. They were designed to fit her concept of two distinct characters. Barbara, left, is a big sister, sedate and "a little bossy"; Suzy, the little sister, is more openly playful. The doll-maker drew her own pattern pieces based on the shapes given here.

Making your own pillow doll pattern would be a great exercise for you at this point, particularly if you know someone who would like to have a Trudy-type friend. Draw some doll shapes freehand on paper until you arrive at one that you think is a likely pattern. Remember to make seam and stuffing allowances in your pattern. If you are a beginner, be prepared to try two or three dolls.

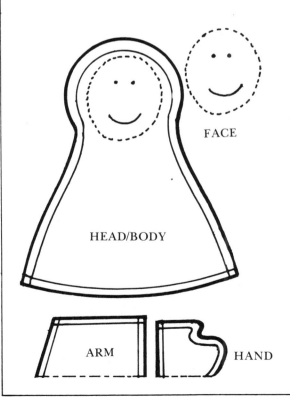

FACE

HEAD/BODY

ARM HAND

Directions for a Trudy Pillow-and-Sock Doll

1. Lightly draw 2 mitten shapes on a double thickness of a cotton sock, using the folded edge as the back edge of the Hand (a). Machine-stitch on the drawn lines, leaving the wrist edge unstitched. Cut out the stitched mittens, turn them right side out and stuff them.

2. Stitch the under-arm seams, turn the Arms right side out, and stuff them. Attach the sock Hands to the Arms (b), with hidden stitches (Blind Hem Stitch, page 51).

3. Clip the Face shape seam margin, turn it to the back, and press it flat (c).

Note: Embroider or appliqué features either at this time, or when the doll is finished. To indent eye buttons, use button and carpet thread and stitch each button to the Face, the Head, a 1"-thick piece of foam padding, and a second scrap of fabric, pulling the thread taut to pinch the foam padding (d).

4. Appliqué the Face shape on the right side of one Head/Body shape (e) with hidden stitches, or by machine. Include a lace or fur trim or yarn hair in the seam if you wish.

5. Pin the finished Arms in position on the front Head/Body shape (f). Stitch the front and back Head/Body shapes together, securing the finished Arms in the seam. Leave a leg opening in the lower edge of the body.

6. Clip all corners and curved seam margins. Turn the Head/Body right side out and stuff it.

7. Stuff 2 small socks. Insert the tops of the stuffed socks into the leg opening in the "skirt" (g). Join the socks and "skirt" with hand stitching through all thicknesses of fabric.

Miss Witch

ISS WITCH is ridiculously small and ineffectual-looking but has a certain presence that belies her size. Always treated with great respect, she had a designated spot under the bed each night for as long as any doll has the right to expect regular attention. She slept with the red sneakers "to keep her happy," as it was explained to me. I don't know exactly what effect Miss Witch had upon Maggie, but I sensed some real urgency in Maggie's quiet communication with that doll.

Underneath her skirt and cape, Miss Witch, shown in color on page 70, is a simple black pillow doll with pointed feet. She has a garish face: appliquéd cheeks, bright-red puckered lips, and a prominent nose. Her eye buttons are cloudy and dark and are drawn toward one another by a concealed thread, pinching wrinkles into her forehead. Her sparse hair (gray mohair yarn) is a mess.

Materials

(Less than ¼ yd of each fabric is required)

Black cotton or cotton knit for lumpy legs, arms, and body
Dark printed or plain cotton for the arms and skirt
Black felt for the hat and cape
Unbleached muslin for the face and hands
A sheer, wild print for the nose and cheeks
A tiny scrap of red fabric for the lips
A few strands of gray mohair yarn for the hair
2 dark pearl shank buttons, ⅜″-diam. for the eyes
Approximately 3 handfuls of polyester fiber, or excelsior for lumpiness
Polyester sewing thread to match the fabrics
Narrow ribbon 12″ long for skirt
Small safety pin or bodkin

Directions

Note: All seams are stitched with the fabric right sides together.

Face and Head

1. Join the 2 sides of the Nose, stitching the center front seam. Clip curved seam margins, turn the piece right side out, and stuff it.

2. Stitch the two Face/Head pieces together, leaving an opening between the dots. Clip the curved seam margins. Turn the Head right side out and stuff it. Close the opening with Whip Stitch (page 51).

3. Position and pin the Cheeks, Lips, and finished Nose on the Face as indicated on the pattern, or as desired, and appliqué them with hidden stitches. Attach button eyes, stitching through the head and pulling the thread taut to indent the face and form wrinkles in the brow. Gather the lips with Running Stitch to form wrinkles.

Arms, Hands, and Legs

4. Stitch each Arm and Leg. Turn the pieces right side out and stuff them.

5. Draw the seam lines for the Hands on the wrong side of the Hand fabric, once for each Hand. Pin each drawn Hand to a second piece of fabric and stitch on the drawn lines (a). Trim the fabric to make narrow seam margins. Clip between the fingers and trim the fingertips to reduce bulk. Turn the Hands right side out and stuff the palms.

6. Attach the Hands to the Arms with hidden stitches.

Body

7. Pin the finished Arms and Legs to the seam margins of the Body Front. Pin the Body Front and Back pieces together with the Arms and Legs tucked inside (b). Stitch around the Body, catching the Arm and Leg end margins in the seam. Leave an opening in one side below the arm. Turn the Body right side out through the side opening. Stuff the Body and close the side seam with hidden stitches.

Attach the Head

8. Pin the Head to the Body Front (c), trying several positions to find the best gesture. Stitch the Head in place with hidden stitches.

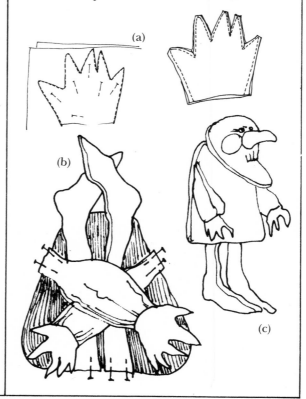

Finishing Touches

9. Stitch a few strands of mohair yarn "hair" to the Head, one or two strands at a time.

10. Make the tall conical hat from felt. Join the 2 sides of the triangular crown and add the brim, stitching by hand with Whip Stitch.

11. Add tiny shoe buckles made from foil to the feet.

12. Make a simple drawstring skirt from a rectangle. Hem the top and bottom edges and join the 2 ends, leaving an opening at the top of the seam. Using a safety pin or a bodkin, thread a narrow ribbon through the top of the skirt to gather it.

13. Wrap a felt shawl or cape around her shoulders and stitch it or snap it together under her chin.

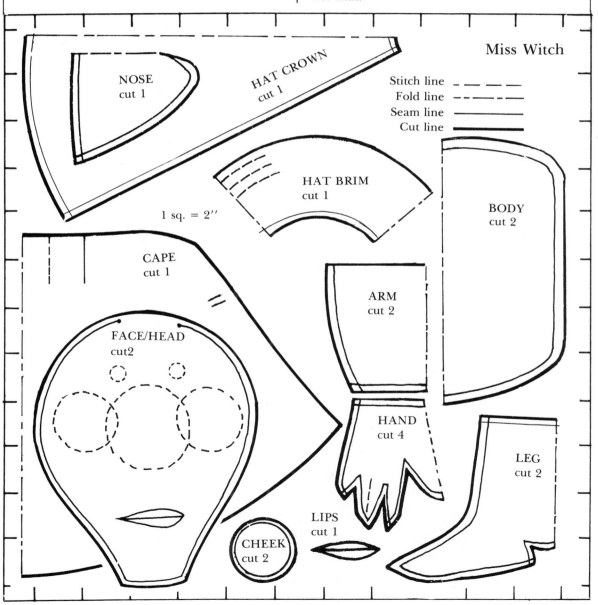

Miss Witch

NOSE
cut 1

HAT CROWN
cut 1

Stitch line — — —
Fold line – – –
Seam line ———
Cut line ▬▬▬

HAT BRIM
cut 1

BODY
cut 2

1 sq. = 2"

CAPE
cut 1

ARM
cut 2

FACE/HEAD
cut2

HAND
cut 4

LEG
cut 2

LIPS
cut 1

CHEEK
cut 2

Granny

GRANNY WAS CREATED on the premise that a little girl ought to be able to act out her fantasies with and confide in a grandma, even when real ones live several states away. She has a lap to sit in and arms to wrap around a child. Her lap has held little tin tea sets, cats, books, and a live caterpillar. This fantasy grandma (page 87) has sufficed nicely from year to year between real Grandma visits.

She is a friendly slipcover over a bentwood chair — a cushion with arms and legs, a shawl and a brooch, and a dear face. Her eye buttons are pale, and her bright lips are wrinkled a little by a few gathering stitches. She wears her rug-yarn hair in a big knot in back, and even grandmas laugh at her funny "old-lady" shoes. I wish I had thought to add nylon stockings over the muslin legs.

The Fairy Godmother (below) is a fancy version of Granny for children who have a grandma close by.

Materials
1½ yds. unbleached muslin for the body, hands, and legs
½ yd. natural-colored canvas or cotton duck for the head
1¾ yds. printed slipcover-weight cotton fabric, for the arms, and dress
1/3 yd. heavyweight black cotton for shoes
16 brown or black eyelets and an eyelet setting tool
18″ black shoelaces
Narrow-strip dark iron-on tape
A pair nylon knee-high straight stockings (optional)
1 skein gray rayon rug yarn for hair
Sobo glue, or other fabric adhesive
Red and magenta embroidery floss for lips
2 eye buttons, approx. ¾″ diam.
Beige embroidery floss for eyebrows
2 small buttons for earrings
2 foam rubber or polyurethane chair seat cushions (optional)
3 lbs. polyester fiber
18″ woven cotton tape for securing Granny to the chair

(pattern appears on page 91)

Preparing the Pattern

Using diagram (a) as a guide, alter the shapes and measurements of the Slipcover Bodice and Bodice patterns to fit your chair back. Change the Body/Lap measurements and length of the Legs pattern as necessary. Measure your chair and add 2″ to the width and overall length measurements to allow for stuffing in the fabric pieces.

Directions

Note: All seams and darts are stitched with the fabric right sides together unless otherwise noted.

Ears

1. Join the two pieces of each Ear, to stitch the outline seam. Clip the curved seam margin, and turn the piece right side out. Stuff the Ears lightly.

2. Top-stitch (through all thicknesses) on the quilting lines.

Nose

3. Join and stitch the Upper and Under Nose pieces. Clip the curved seam margin, and turn the piece right side out.

Head

4. Stitch Face darts A, and Head Back darts B.

5. Embroider the lips, using 2 shades of magenta, red, or pink, using the darker for the upper lip.

6. Aligning the raw edges, place the finished Ears over the Face, and stitch them to the seam margin (b).

7. Place the Head Back over the Face and stitch the outline seam, including the Ears in the seam, and leaving an opening between the dots.

8. Turn the Head right side out and stuff it. Close the opening with hidden stitches.

9. Attach the Nose with hidden stitches, stuffing it as you go.

10. Indent nostrils and each side of the lips with tiny stitches, catching the stuffing underneath. Make a few gathering stitches crosswise between the lips.

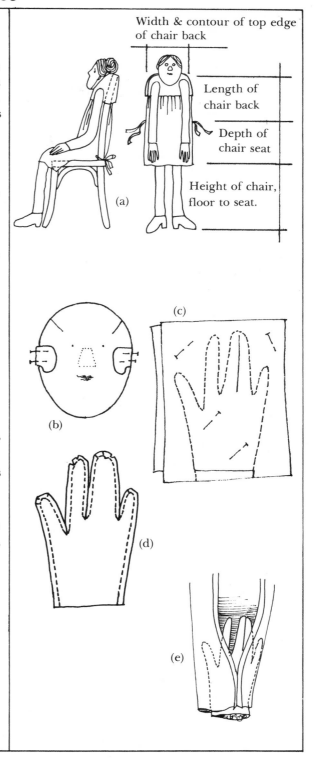

(a) Width & contour of top edge of chair back / Length of chair back / Depth of chair seat / Height of chair, floor to seat.

(b)

(c)

(d)

(e)

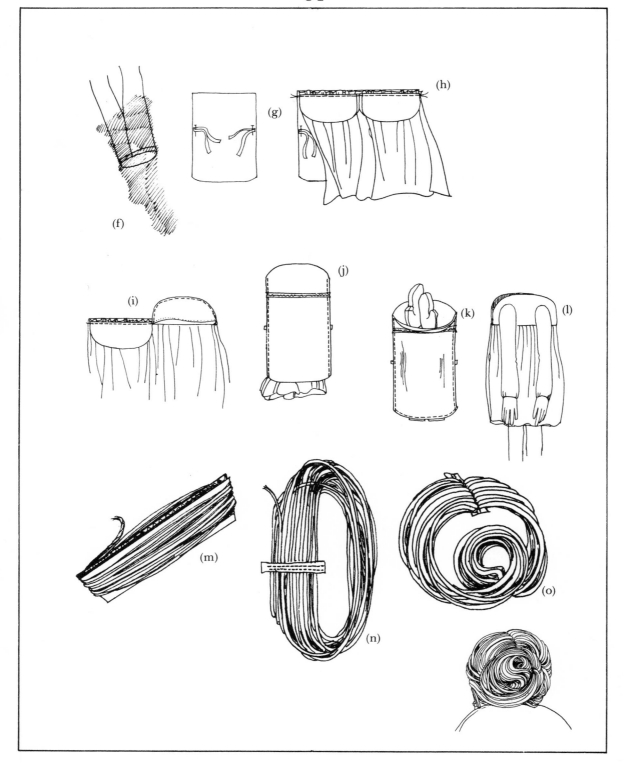

11. Attach eye buttons with button and carpet thread and a sailmaker's needle, sewing through all thicknesses to indent the Face. Indentations at the back of the Head will be covered by rug yarn hair.

12. Embroider a few eyebrow stitches above the eyes.

Hands

13. Draw the Hand seam lines lightly with pencil on the wrong side of the fabric, once for each hand.

14. Pin the drawings to two more pieces of Hand fabric (right sides together, drawing side up). Stitch on the drawn lines with very short machine stitches (c).

15. When both Hands are stitched, cut them out, leaving ¼" margins around the stitching. Clip curved edges and between all but the 2 middle fingers (d). Turn the Hands right side out and stuff them. Top stitch between the 2 middle fingers on each hand.

Sleeves (arms)

16. Make long Running or machine stitches in the Sleeve tops between dots, but do not gather them.

17. Fold each Sleeve, right sides together, to stitch from the wrist edge to the dot *only.*

Join Hands and Sleeves

18. Insert the finished Hands into the Sleeves, right sides together, matching wrist edges, and with Sleeve seams at the palms of the hands (e).

19. With Running Stitch, gather the wrist edge of each Sleeve to fit the stuffed Hand, and join the Sleeves and Hands with hidden Running Stitch.

20. With a hand still inside each sleeve, close the Sleeve seam (by machine).

21. Turn the Sleeves right side out. Stuff them and pull the top gathers taut to close them.

Shoes

22. Use iron-on bonding material or Sobo glue to attach interfacings to the eyelet facings. Fold eyelet facings under and stitch them to the shoe.

23. Use an eyelet setting tool to set eyelets (according to the manufacturer's directions).

24. Fold the Shoe (right side in), to stitch seam C, breaking the thread to skip over dart D, and continue to the center back fold. Fold seam C onto itself to stitch toe dart D, dart E, and heel darts F and G. Trim the dart margins, and clip curved seam margins and the apex of the instep. When both Shoes are made, turn them right side out and stuff the toes and heels only.

Legs

25. Fold the Legs and stitch between the dots. Note: If stockings are to be used, turn the Legs right side out, and slip the stockings over them at this time, matching the stocking and Leg ankle areas. Apply Sobo glue through the stockings to the ankle margins of the Legs (f). When the glue is dry, cut off the stocking feet. Turn the Legs inside out.

Join Shoes and Legs

26. Insert the finished, partially stuffed Shoes, matching the Shoe center back to the Leg seam, and aligning ankle edges. Join the Shoes and Legs by hand with small Running Stitch or by machine.

27. With the Shoes still inside the Legs, and being careful not to catch them in the seams, stitch the Leg seams. Turn the Legs right side out. Stuff the Shoes firmly as you close them with shoelaces.

28. Stuff the Legs and pull the stockings up over them.

Lap, Bodice, and Skirt

29. With right sides together, join Skirt Front and Back at one side, leaving a 1" opening between dots for the tie tapes (which tie Granny to the chair).

30. With Running Stitch, gather the top edge of the Skirt, and pull the gathers to 25" (or double the width of the Bodice piece for your chair).

31. Fold the 20" tapes in half and pin them into place on each side of the Lap about 13" (or your

chair seat depth) from the lower edge (g).

32. Join the Lap Front and Back at one side, catching the tie tapes in the seam.

33. Pin the Bodice Front and Back, right sides together, to stitch one side seam only.

Join Skirt, Lap, and Bodice

34. Place the gathered Skirt over the Lap Front and Back, right sides up, and Bodice Front and Back over them, wrong sides up, aligning the top edges (h). Stitch through all thicknesses.

35. Hem the straight edge of the bodice Slip Cover. Stitch the Slip cover to the Bodice Back seam margin with both pieces right side up (i).

36. Fold the Skirt right sides together to stitch the remaining side seam, leaving an opening between the dots for the tape ties, as before.

37. Fold the Bodice and Lap right sides together, tucking the skirt inside. Stitch the Lap side seam and both Bodice side seams (j).

Attach Legs and Arms

38. Insert the finished, stuffed legs upward into the body, Shoe heels facing the Body back. Tuck the skirt edge inside the body. Pin, then stitch the lower edge seam of the Lap, catching the upper edge of the Legs in the seam (k). Turn the piece right side out.

39. Position the finished, stuffed Arms on the Bodice front (1), and attach them with button and carpet thread and hidden stitches.

40. Pull the tie tapes out through the holes in the Skirt. Stuff the Bodice and Lap with batting alone, or foam padding and polyester batting.

Finish the Body

41. Close the upper Bodice seam by hand with hidden stitches.

42. Hem the Skirt.

Attach the Head

43. Pin the finished Head into position on the Bodice and stitch it with button and carpet thread and a sailmaker's or curved upholstery needle.

Hair

44. Wind about 80 loops of rug yarn over a 19''-long cardboard (m).

45. Stitch one section of the loops onto an 8''-long fabric strip, ½'' wide, with very short machine stitches (n).

46. Glue the strip to the center top of Granny's head. Arrange the yarn hair loop in a twist as desired and secure it with Sobo glue and Whip Stitch (o). Add a knot or a coiled braid of the leftover yarn if desired.

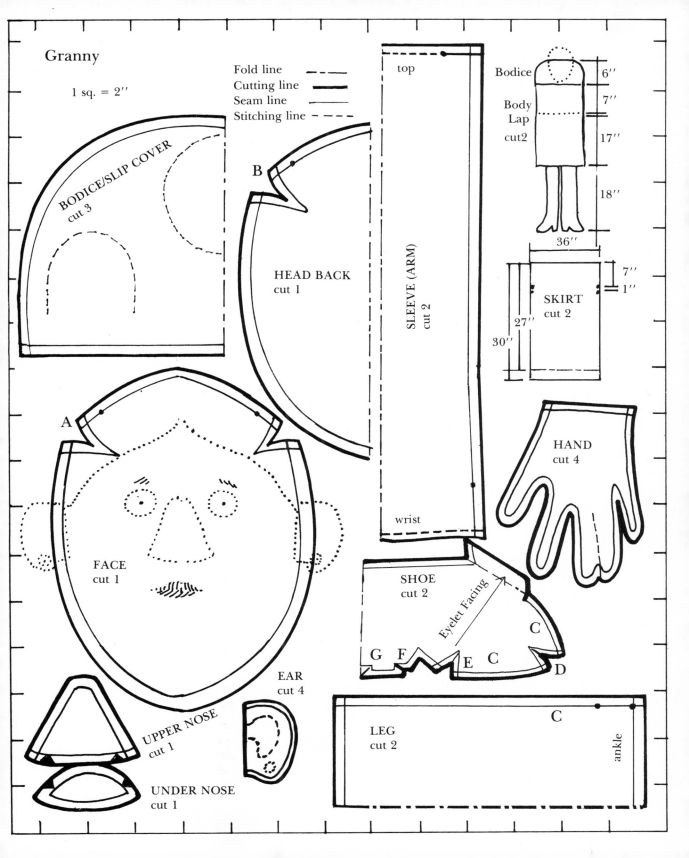

Toad

FTER the first toad is made, this can quickly become a less-than-two-hour project. The possible characters within these pattern shapes are far-ranging, as toys, table art, or deck cushions. When I was a very small child, a black velveteen, great and ominous frog crouched on the patterned carpet at my grandmother's house. It had giant orange satin eyes, and stubby fingers that were sewn together under the chin. It is gone with my childhood, but the hours I must have spent with it had their influence.

We have discussed Maggie's Toad at some length (page 38). He is pictured on page 88. He is made of quilted cotton and flowered chintz and stuffed with beans, shredded polyurethane foam, and polyester fiber. He feels bumpy, cool, and slick underneath and has hard, heavy toes. He is weighted so that, when he's dropped, he lands right side up and bounces a little. He is 8 inches long, 12 inches around.

The smaller toad, Rosebud, is made from printed duck and polished cotton. It has beady, glove-button eyes.

Materials

Since these toads require so little in the way of materials, I suggest you simply enlarge the pattern to a size you like, then choose 2 or 3 remnants to fit the pattern shapes, and begin.

You will need stuffing and eye beads or buttons.

Directions

1. Stitch dart A in the Head and dart B in the Back.

2. Join the Head and Back at seam C, aligning darts A and B.

3. Join the Chin and Head, and the Belly and Back, around the outer edge seam line, leaving the opening between the Chin and Belly for turning and stuffing. Clip curved seam margins. Turn the piece right side out and stuff it with polyester fiber, shredded foam rubber, and beans. Close the Chin/Belly seam with hidden stitches (Blind Hem Stitch, page 51).

4. With a pencil, lightly draw the foot seam line on the wrong side of one piece of fabric for each Leg.

Pin that piece to the second piece of fabric (for each Leg and foot) and stitch on the drawn lines with short machine stitches, leaving an opening between the dots (a). Trim around the toes, leaving narrow seam margins. Clip the curved seam margins and between the toes. Turn the Legs right side out.

5. Stuff the toes with beans and the Legs with shredded foam rubber or polyester fiber, pinching a "joint" in each Hind Leg with a few stitches (b).

6. Form the pleats in the Eye Fronts, securing them with stitches in the seam margins (c). Stitch dart D in each Eye Back. Join the Eye Fronts to the Eye Backs around curved top and sides. Turn right sides out and stuff the Eye sockets with polyester fiber.

7. Attach the Eye sockets to the Head with hidden stitches. Add eye beads between the "eyelids," catching the stuffing in the stitches to indent the beads slightly.

8. Attach the Legs as indicated on the pattern, using heavy-duty thread and Overcast Stitch (page 51).

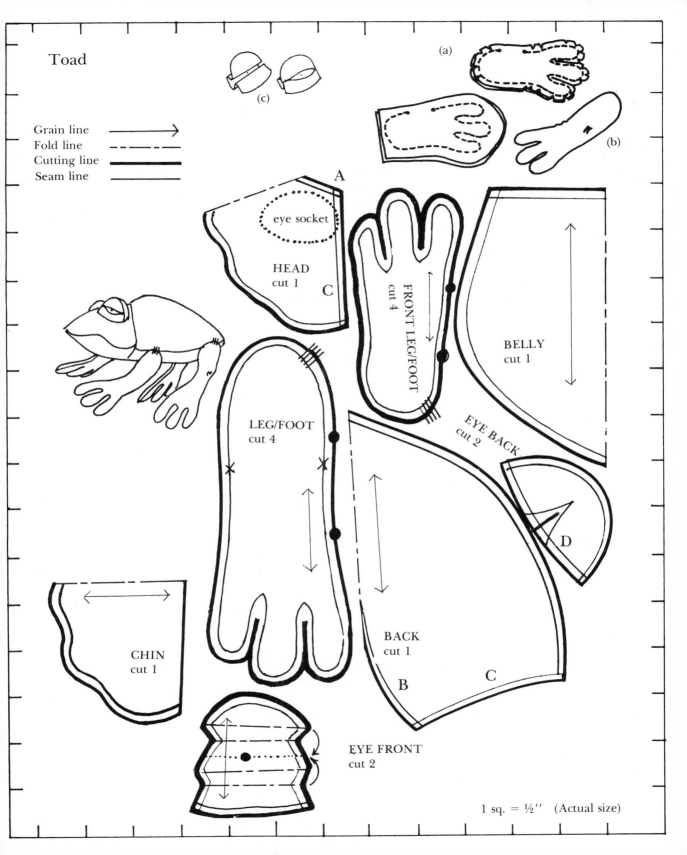

Toad

Grain line ——————→
Fold line — — — — —
Cutting line ▬▬▬▬▬
Seam line ————————

(a)

(b)

(c)

A

eye socket

HEAD
cut 1

C

FRONT LEG/FOOT
cut 4

BELLY
cut 1

LEG/FOOT
cut 4

EYE BACK
cut 2

D

CHIN
cut 1

BACK
cut 1

B   C

EYE FRONT
cut 2

1 sq. = ½'' (Actual size)

Bear

THIS BEAR (page 89) is not a teddy bear or the work of a taxidermist. But he *is* excitingly believable, by his size, furry texture, cool leather nose and foot pads, and amber button eyes that follow your movement around him. He readily takes a number of imagination-provoking positions, plays pat-a-cake like the most entertaining zoo bears I've seen, and has a barely manageable, but manageable, bulk that seems to delight and challenge small people. Bear weighs nineteen pounds and stands five feet tall. Like the most successful teddy bear, he has that wonderful ability to reflect people moods with perfect timing. He has character.

This is a project for any beginner or intermediate in the craft of machine sewing. The shapes are perhaps confusing to look at, but in fact go together very simply. There are no tricky or difficult seams, no easing-together of edges of unequal length, no laborious hand-stitching through great bulk. The stuffing is simply dumped and tamped into a presewn bearskin bag. The hand-stitched closing seam is at the chest — easily accessible. The only tedium, if you classify hand sewing as tedious, is in stitching the leather foot pads (palms and toes) to the unfinished feet, padding them as you go.

Materials

4⅓ yds. suitable long-pile fabric (fake fur), 60″ wide
Polyester thread
2 amber-colored round shank buttons
1 sq. ft. soft, dark 2½-oz. leather
Polyester buttonhole twist thread
Between needle
Sailmaker's needle
Polyurethane foam pad, 12″ × 20″, ½″ thick
12″ x 24″ muslin
Curved upholstery needle
Button and carpet thread
18 lbs. polyester fiber

Directions

Note: An electric hair trimmer will "shear" the feet, inner ears, and muzzle quickly and more evenly than fabric shears. Refer to page 53 for special considerations in sewing with fake fur.

Stitch all seams and darts with the fabric right sides together.

Tail

1. Join the Upper and Lower Tail pieces around seam line B. Turn the piece right side out and stuff it. Close the opening with top stitching.

Foot Pads

2. Shear the shaded Foot areas indicated on the pattern.

3. Pin the leather Foot Pad palms and toes in position on the corresponding right and left Front Legs and Hind Foot Soles. Stitch with Blind Hem or Whip Stitch, using a between needle and buttonhole twist thread. Use Back Stitch between joined areas. Pad the palms and toes as you go (a).

Front Legs

4. Stitch darts C, D, E, and F. Bring small o's and large O's together with a few stitches for an inner elbow crease. Stitch "elbow" seams G and outer-leg seams H, in that order (b).

Hind Legs

5. Stitch darts I, J, and K.

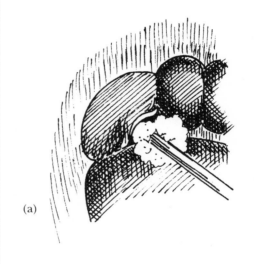

(a)

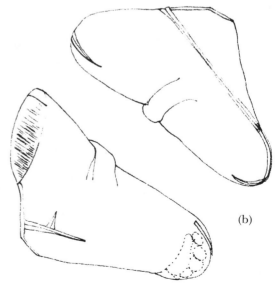

(b)

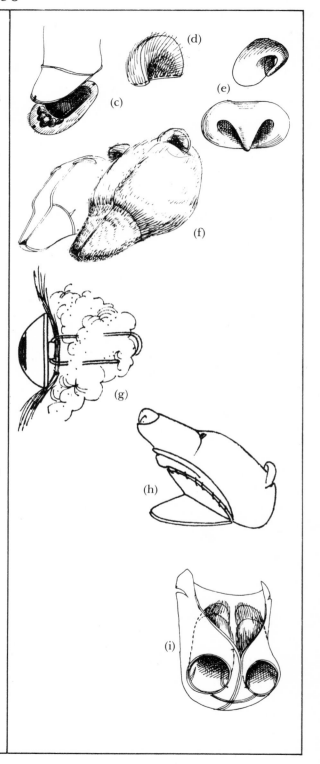

6. Matching triangles, pin and then stitch seams L to join the Upper Foot pieces to the corresponding right or left Hind Leg front.

7. Stitch the leg inseams M.

8. Matching squares, join the finished Foot Soles to the corresponding right or left Hind Legs around seams N (c).

9. Turn the Front and Hind Legs right side out, but do not stuff them.

Ears

10. Shear the Inner Ear pieces. Join the Inner and Outer Ear pieces around seamline O. Turn the Ears right side out.

11. Fold each Ear, bringing the side seam to the large dot, top-stitching the raw edges to close the Ear and secure the fold (d).

Nose

12. Fold the leather Nose piece to stitch the center seam P. Turn the piece right side out.

13. Fold and pin the center fold line over seam P, matching small dots (e).

Head

14. Stitch the cheek darts Q and side-back darts R. Make long Running stitches between the small dots at each jaw edge, and gather them to measure 2''.

15. Shear the shaded Muzzle areas as indicated on the pattern.

16. Matching triangles, stitch the Head cheek areas to the Muzzle pieces at seams S.

17. Matching squares and Ear slots, pin, then stitch the Brow/Muzzle center strip to the Head and Muzzle pieces at side-front seams T.

18. Insert and pin the finished Ears into the Ear slots, matching the large dots. Stitch the Ears and close the slots by hand with a between needle, buttonhole twist thread and Cobbler's or Back Stitch through all thicknesses.

19. Stitch seam U to close the Muzzle. (The nose end is left open.) Turn the Head right side out (f), and stuff the Muzzle.

20. Stuff the leather Nose. Pin the Nose in place on the Muzzle, and stitch it with a between needle and buttonhole twist thread with hidden stitches.

21. Matching triangles, stitch the Neck Gusset to the Head front at seam V.

22. Partially stuff the Head center front area. Attach the eye buttons with polyester buttonhole twist thread, catching the stuffing behind the eyes (g), and pulling the thread taut to indent the Head slightly.

23. Stuff the Head. Fold the Neck Gusset out of the way. Whip Stitch one side of the Foam Neck Pad to the seam margin at Head front seam V (h). (This pad keeps the head stuffing from falling into the gusset area.) Use button and carpet thread and a sailmaker's needle.

Body

24. Stitch the Body center back seam, and dart W across it. Insert the finished Tail from the fur side (inside), into the Tail slot. Attach the Tail with Cobbler's Stitch, a sailmaker's needle, and buttonhole twist thread through all thicknesses.

25. Stitch the lower half of the Body center front seam and dart X across it.

26. Insert the finished, unstuffed Hind Legs into the corresponding right and left Leg Holes from inside the Body (i). Match the Leg inseams to the triangles at the front (belly) edge of the Leg Holes. Working from the outside, use Cobbler's or Back Stitch, a sailmaker's needle and buttonhole twist thread to attach the Hind Legs around the Leg Holes.

27. Stuff the Legs, using one pound plus one handful of polyester fiber for each Leg. Leave the thighs only sparsely stuffed for mobility. Block the Leg openings with muslin circles Whip stitched to the seam margins. Use the hind leg hole seam line on the pattern as a cutting guide for the muslin circles.

28. Fold the Front Leg Hole flaps to the outside. Insert the Front Legs from inside the Body into the corresponding right and left Leg Holes, matching triangles. Stitch as for the Hind Legs.

29. Continue closing the Body center front seam to the neck edge. Stitch dart Y across the center front seam. Stitch the shoulder darts Z.

Attach the Head

30. Pin the back of the Head to the Body Back, (right sides together), aligning the triangle and center back seam. Stitch by machine, or by hand with a between needle, buttonhole twist thread, and Cobbler's or Back Stitch (j).

31. Turn the Body right side out and place it in a seated position. Stuff the Body and Front Legs, leaving the upper areas of the Front Legs only sparsely stuffed for mobility.

32. Attach the foam Neck Pad flap to the Body Front seam margin with Whip Stitch.

33. Stitch the Neck Gusset into place on the Body Front, folding the seam margin to the inside. Use a between needle, buttonhole twist thread, and Blind Hem Stitch.

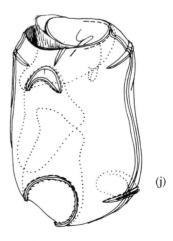

(j)

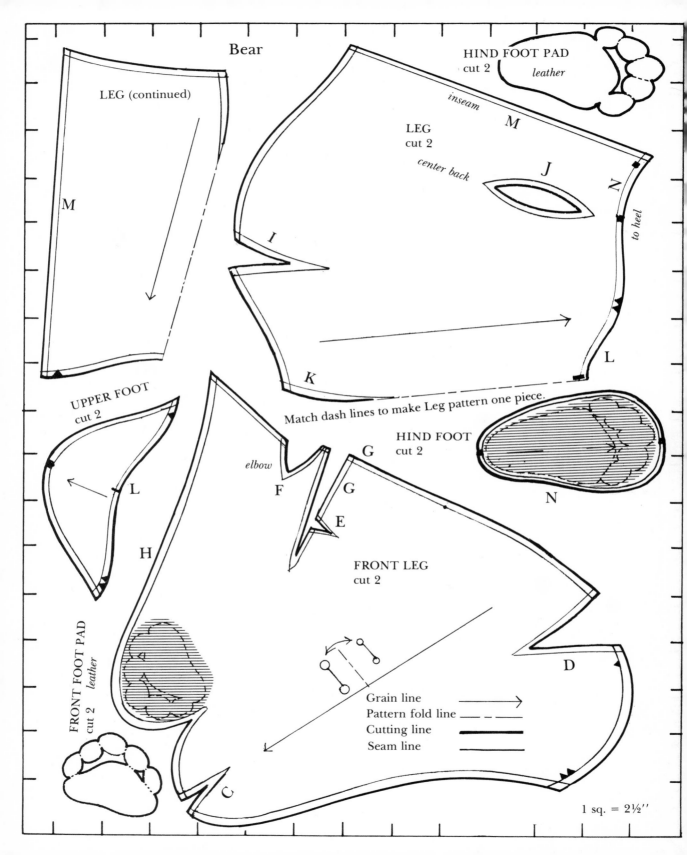

Bear

LEG (continued)

M

HIND FOOT PAD
cut 2

leather

inseam

M

LEG
cut 2

center back

J

N

to heel

I

L

K

UPPER FOOT
cut 2

Match dash lines to make Leg pattern one piece.

HIND FOOT
cut 2

L

elbow

F

G

G

N

E

H

FRONT LEG
cut 2

FRONT FOOT PAD
cut 2 *leather*

D

Grain line
Pattern fold line
Cutting line
Seam line

C

1 sq. = 2½″

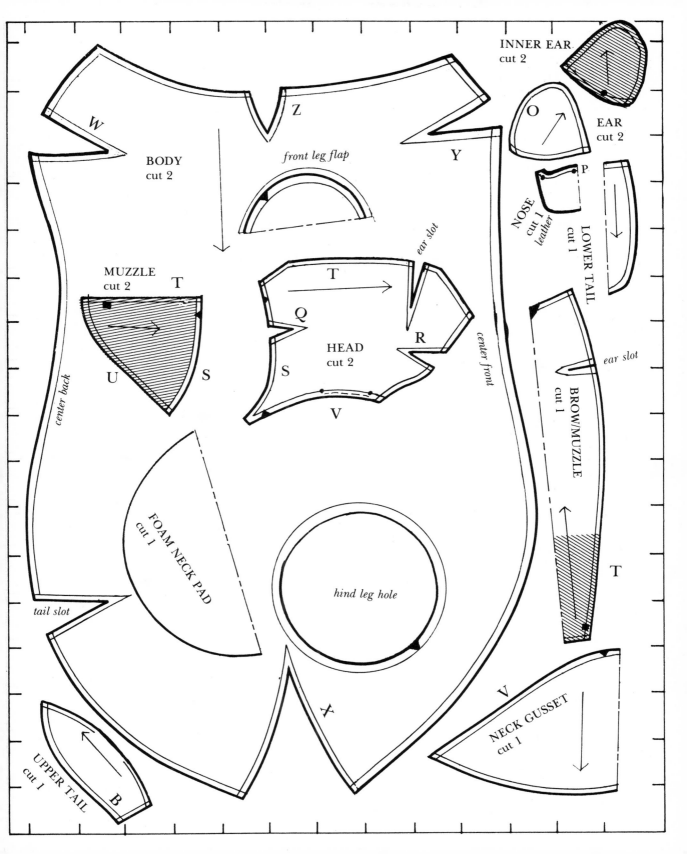

Seal Slider

THIS GREAT BLUE SEAL (page 90) is a sled, designed for kids and for fun. Nylon ski-wear fabric over foam rubber makes it glide over powder where other sleds bog. Body "english" steers it, and spills are as much fun as the ride. It is lightweight and can't hurt anyone at the bottom of the hill. This is probably the only sled that's also entertaining on the uphill trip.

The Seal Slider is designed for play. There are no unnecessary seams to split, and none on the sliding surface of the belly. The flippers are filled with polyurethane foam padding and hand-quilted. A thick foam rubber pad around a core of polyester fiber retains the body shape even under great abuse. The Seal Slider is 48 inches long, plus flippers, and 46 inches around the middle.

Materials

2½ yds. nylon ski-wear fabric
Nylon thread
Button and carpet thread
Heavy-duty polyester thread
Foam rubber padding, 48″ × 30″, 2″ thick
1 polyurethane foam pad, 34″ × 20″, ¼″ thick
2 polyurethane chair pads, each 15″ × 17″, 1″ thick
Polyester buttonhole twist thread
Sailmaker's or other long needle
5 lbs. polyester fiber
2 black buttons, 1″ diam.
2 buttons, 1″ – 1½″ diam. (for attaching flippers inside the body)
Curved upholstery needle

Directions

Note: All nylon fabric seams and darts are stitched with the right sides together. Make Butt Seams in the foam padding with button and carpet thread, a sailmaker's needle, and Whip Stitch (a).

Head

1. Stitch nylon Head pieces together on seam line A, breaking the thread to skip over "mouth" dart B.

2. Make long Running stitches on seam line A between darts B and C, and gather them to measure 1½″.

(pattern begins on page 102)

3. Fold seam A onto itself to stitch darts B and C across it. Clip curved seam margins and trim darts.

4. Whip-stitch darts D in the Head Padding.

5. Bend the Head Padding to stitch seam E.

6. Stitch seam F on the padding Collar. Join the Head and Collar padding at seam G with a few widely spaced Whip stitches.

7. Match the "nose" dart C to the Head Padding "nose" point (b), and fold the nylon Head into position over the padding (c). Make "nostrils" at each side of nose dart C, stitching through the nylon and the padding with buttonhole twist thread and a sailmaker's needle.

8. Make "ear" indentations and attach eye buttons in the same manner. Stuff the Head with polyester fiber.

Flippers
9. Stitch each Side and Rear Flipper around the outer seam line, leaving an opening between dots for turning and stuffing. Clip curved seam margins and turn the pieces right side out.

10. Insert Flipper Padding pieces into corresponding nylon Flippers. Close only the Front Flipper openings, using nylon or heavy-duty polyester thread and hidden stitches (Blind Hem Stitch).

11. Draw quilting lines with tailor's chalk on the top side of each Flipper or pin them without drawn lines. Use a sailmaker's needle and buttonhole twist thread to quilt the Flipper through all thicknesses with Cobbler's Stitch.

12. Match the Rear Flippers, right sides together. Stitching through all thicknesses, join the flippers at the 3 dots (d).

13. Shape each Rear Flipper, stitching the side edges together (e). Create a sharp bend 3″ from the Body end, bringing the triangles together with a curved upholstery needle, buttonhole twist thread, and Whip Stitch (f).

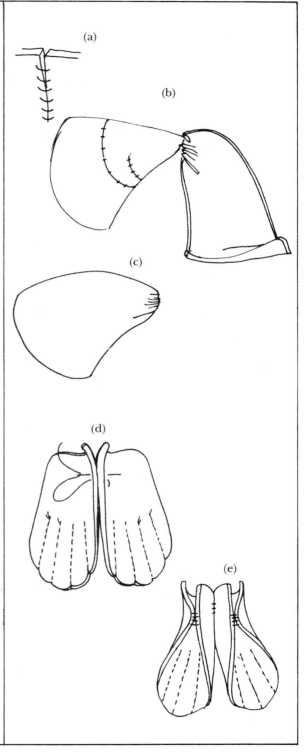

Body

14. Join Belly seam H; join Body Back seam I. Join the nylon Body Back and Belly pieces at seams J, leaving an opening between dots for the Rear Flippers. Turn the Body right side out.

15. Insert the Belly and Back Padding pieces through the neck opening (g).

Attach the Flippers

16. Insert the open ends of the finished Rear Flippers into the rear Body opening. Working from the outside, stitch the Flippers to the Body with nylon thread and hidden stitches, folding the Body raw edges to the inside as you stitch.

17. Attach the finished Side Flippers to the Body from the outside, stitching through all thicknesses and through large buttons on the inside to keep the thread from tearing through the foam (h).

Finishing

18. Stuff the Body densely with polyester fiber.

19. Pin the finished, stuffed Head in position on the Body, folding the raw edges to the inside. Stitch with Blind Hem Stitch, nylon thread, and a regular sewing needle.

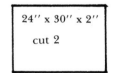

24″ x 30″ x 2″

cut 2

Belly & Back Padding (foam)

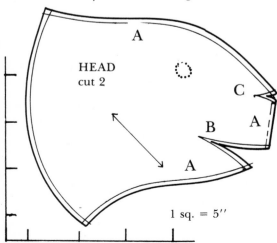

A

HEAD
cut 2

C

B

A

A

A

1 sq. = 5″

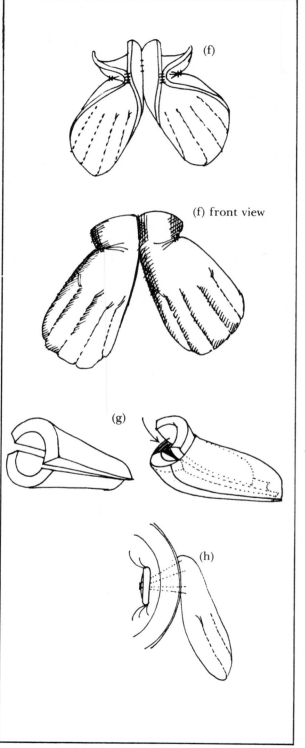

(f)

(f) front view

(g)

(h)

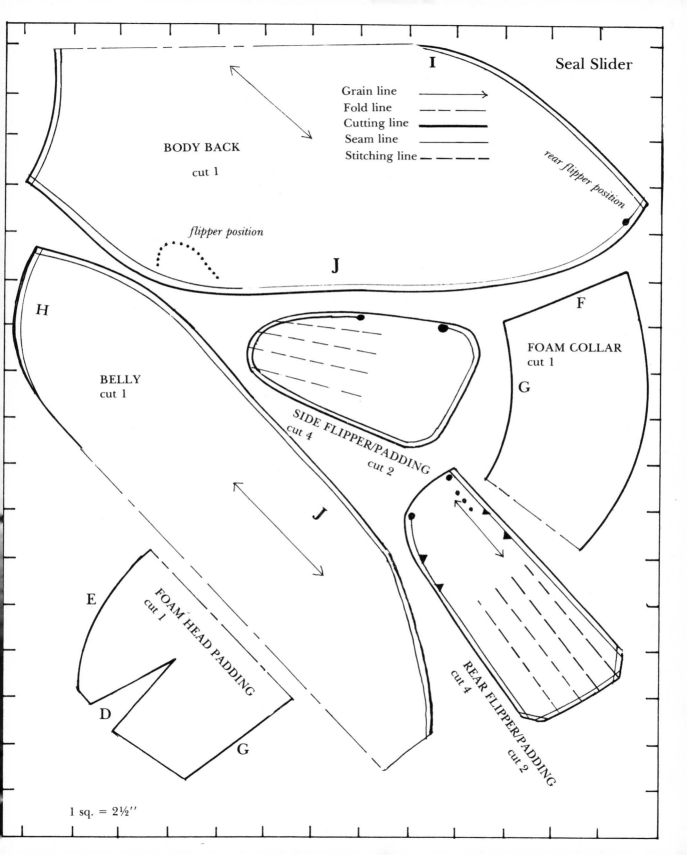

Seal Slider

I

Grain line
Fold line
Cutting line
Seam line
Stitching line

BODY BACK

cut 1

rear flipper position

flipper position

J

H

F

FOAM COLLAR
cut 1

G

BELLY
cut 1

SIDE FLIPPER/PADDING
cut 4
cut 2

J

E

FOAM HEAD PADDING
cut 1

D

G

REAR FLIPPER/PADDING
cut 4
cut 2

1 sq. = 2½''

Body Changers: Sewn Sculpture Costume

SEWN SCULPTURE can be used impressively in theatrical costumes in the form of masks or complete body coverings. With the human body as an armature, three-dimensional sewn forms can move; the symbolic nuances multiply.

Although this cloth-and-stitches folk art lends itself easily to humorous costumes, it has great aesthetic possibilities. The Japanese Kabuki theater borrowed its highly formalized shapes and actions from the earlier Joururi theater in which dramas were acted out by large puppets.

Padding, oversized masks, and high-soled foot gear have long been used in theater to increase the dramatic impact of characters and to enable actors to portray with more realism beasts, gods, heroes, and demons. The addition of a dummy character attached to a performer is recorded in a seventeenth-century costume design: a woman carrying a basket with a man in it on her back. The performer is the man in the basket, who also provides the woman's legs and feet.

Perhaps the two most startling possibilities of the sewn sculpture costume are in the naturalism offered by cloth textures and stuffed forms and in the unexpected scale or dramatic distortion it may provide, which is made even more dramatic by those realistic qualities of sewn cloth forms.

The Muppets of television fame are an excellent contemporary example of exciting and believable sewn sculpture costumes.

A Crowd of Ogres

AN INFORMAL COSTUME for one-time occasions can be a sewn sketch. A Halloween costume, for example, usually doesn't warrant a great deal of time spent in its construction. In fact, sometimes the more spontaneous the costume, the more fun it can be for everyone involved in its creation and its debut.

Any of the five heads in this crowd costume (pages 107, 108) may be altered for use as a mask to combine with a pinned-together ragbag costume. Having made the Crowd of Ogres, I admit it is an undertaking, not for any complexity of its parts, but for the number of parts. I think it's a great idea, but I wouldn't do it for one night of trick-or-treat. It warrants at least an annual parade, or party, or theatrical performance.

This costume lurches along, reaching out in all directions, legs swinging and bumping one another. The central face (the mask) is not easily picked out of the crowd, nor are the real arms and hands, which gives a person an uneasy moment trying to direct conversation.

The mask, with another head in back, is easily slipped on and off, and even fits over glasses. A tube cape of black felt, gathered by a drawstring at the neck, is worn over clothing. The cape holds all the heads and arms of the crowd. The wearer's forearms fit through real sleeves in the front of the cape and into a pair of garden gloves (or any old gloves). The dangling legs, matched pairs, coincide with the various faces and arms spaced around the cape, and hang from a coat-hanger-wire ring tied hoop-skirt fashion to a belt around the waist of the wearer. The heads are stuffed with polyester fiber, crumpled netting, or tissue paper. The lumpy legs and arms are stuffed with wadded newspaper. The fabrics in this example are burlap, hairy fake furs, and textured knits.

All sorts of crowds may be made in this manner. Your crowd may be fierce ogres or Disney dwarfs or even a humorous if slightly grotesque dither of ladies at an afternoon tea.

Materials for Each Ogre
Approx. 1¼ yds. fabric for the Face, Head Back, Arms, Hands, and Legs; scraps for the inner mouth, ears, and horns; fake fur scraps for a beard, a mustache, eyebrows, or hair
Assorted oblong beads or Styrofoam pieces for teeth
2 Buttons for eyes
Button and carpet thread and a large needle
Machine- and hand-sewing thread
Sobo glue (optional)

Polyurethane foam padding, ½" thick (mask only)
A few sq. in. iron-on cloth or interfacing (mask only)
1 lb. polyester fiber or other lightweight stuffing material
Miscellaneous stuffing materials: newspaper, tissue, plastic bags, Styrofoam pellets

Additional materials
2 yds. black felt for Cape and Sleeves
(pattern begins on page 112)

1 yd. heavy cord for a drawstring
Coat-hanger-wire ring, 20″ diam.
Regular belt to fit the wearer's waist

Directions

Note: Cut each Ear, Horn, Hand, Leg, and Arm separately rather than from 4 thicknesses of fabric. Cut each side of the face separately rather than with a center fold. Just try to copy the first side in reverse; the lack of symmetry will add character and excitement to the piece. Seams need not match perfectly; ease and tuck them as necessary for fit and gesture. All darts and seams are stitched with the fabric right sides together unless otherwise noted.

Head I (Mask)

1. Fit the Face pattern to the wearer, marking the placement and size of the eye holes. Back the eye areas with iron-on interfacing before cutting the eye holes.

2. Stitch the 2 sides of each Ear together. Turn the Ears right side out and stuff them lightly. Machine-stitch on the quilting lines (through all thicknesses). Fold and stitch the top corner of each Ear to meet the dot (a).

3. Stitch the crown center and side-center darts A and side darts B. Form the Crown pleats and secure them with top stitching in the side seam margins.

4. Make Running-Stitch gathers in the end of the Nose to fit the Under Nose piece, and join the two pieces (b).

5. Form lip pleats D, E, and F on Mouth. Stuff the lips (c). Attach teeth by stitching vertically through the 2 lips and a "tooth" bead (d).

6. Join the Mouth and Under Nose at seam lines G.

7. Attach the Nose and Mouth piece to the Face stitching around seam H.

8. Working from the wrong side, attach the Nose (foam) Backing to the seam margins alongside the nose, stuffing the nose as you close it (e). Use button and carpet thread and Whip Stitch.

9. Stitch the Beard center dart, and attach the Beard to the outer edge of the Face by machine.

10. Stitch the center dart in the Face Backing, using button and carpet thread and Whip Stitch. Join the Backing and the Face at the lower and side edges with long Running stitches. Stuff the Face.

11. Join the Backing and the Face at the lower rims of the eye holes, the bridge of the nose, and above the nostrils as marked by x's on the pattern.

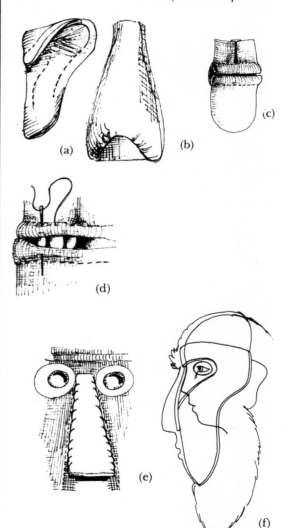

(a)   (b)   (c)

(d)

(e)   (f)

12. Now fit the mask to the wearer to adjust the foam padding for comfort and visibility, leaving adequate breathing space (f).

13. Make Running stitches on the center line of each Horn, and gather them to measure 4″. Stitch the outer edge I. Clip the seam margins. Turn the Horns right side out and stuff them.

14. Folding the raw edges under as you stitch, attach the Horns to the Face with hidden stitches.

15. Position and attach the Ears with Whip Stitch, working from the back (g), then stitching the upper folded edges back (h).

16. Attach fake fur Eyebrows with Whip Stitch.

Head II (Back of Mask)

1. Stitch the Inner Mouth to the Lower Lip at seam lines A, and to the upper lip edge of the Face at seam lines B (i).

2. Stitch the Lower Lip to the Chin at seam lines C.

3. Stitch the Head to the Face around the outer edge, skipping over darts D, and leaving an opening between dots for turning.

4. Fold the stitched outer seam onto itself to stitch darts D. Turn the Head right side out, stuff it, and close the openings.

5. With a few stitches through all thicknesses, join the Inner Mouth and upper lip of the Face at x's. Use button and carpet thread.

6. Shape the Lower Lip in the same manner (j).

7. Stitch through the Styrofoam "teeth" to attach them to the Inner Mouth (k).

8. Fold the Nose to stitch lower seam E. Turn the piece right side out to bring dots together and stitch.

9. Position the Nose on the Face, folding the raw edges under, and stitch with hidden stitches.

10. Stitch the long side of each Horn. Clip the curved seam margins. Turn the Horns right side out and stuff them. Attach the Horns to the Head with hidden stitches.

11. Make a central pleat in each Ear. Attach the Ears to the Head with Whip Stitch.

12. Attach eye buttons and furry Eye Backings with button and carpet thread, stitching through the head with a long needle to indent it slightly.

13. Join the 2 ends of the Neck. Working from the outside of the piece, attach the Neck to the Head with button and carpet thread and hidden stitches.

14. Join the Crown of Head I to the upper edge of the Neck (l).

Head III (Head Within a Head)

1. Join the Face and Head Back pieces around the outer edge, leaving an opening between the dots. Turn the head right side out, stuff it, and close the opening.

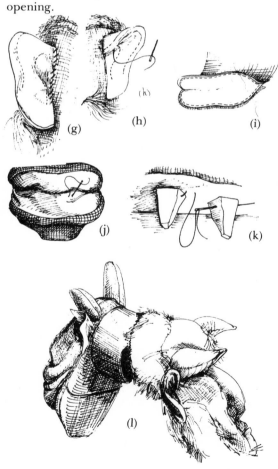

(g) (h) (h) (i)

(j) (k)

(l)

2. Stitch the upper and lobe Ear seams. Turn the Ears right side out and stuff them. Stitch through all thicknesses on the quilting lines. Attach the Ears with hidden stitches.

3. Form the Lips tube, right side out. Stuff it and join the ends with hidden stitches (m). Attach the seam margin to the Face (n).

4. Stitch the Nose center dart A. Fold nostrils on center lines to stitch seams B (o). Indent the nostrils and stuff the Nose. Fold the raw edges under as you stitch the Nose in place with hidden stitches.

5. Appliqué eye pieces to the Face, and attach eye buttons.

Tiny Head

6. Form and top-stitch the lip pleats of the Tiny Face (p).

7. Join the Face and Head Back around the outer edges. Cut a slot in the back. Turn the Head right side out and stuff it through the slot.

8. Make and attach the Nose as above (step 4).

9. Stitch Styrofoam "teeth" to the mouth as in Head II, step 7.

10. Stitch the eye buttons in place, pulling the thread taut to indent the Face.

11. Insert the Tiny Head into the large mouth and secure it with Sobo glue or a few hidden stitches.

Head IV (Yellow)

1. Stitch the Face center dart A.

2. On the right side of the fabric, bring the small dot to the large dot to make a folded brow.

3. Stitch cheek darts B.

4. Gather the jaw edges with Long Running stitches.

5. Form the upper lip pleats C and D, bringing small x's to large X's (q).

6. Attach the chin and mouth piece to the Face, stitching seams F (r).

7. Form pleats in the Ears and secure them with top stitching. Pin the Ears to the Face, raw edges together (s).

8. Stitch center dart G and side darts H in the Head Back.

9. Join the Head Back and Face around the outer edge, including the Ears in the seam, and leaving an opening between dots. Turn the Head right side out and stuff it. Close the opening with hidden stitches.

10. Form the Nose as for Head III, step 4. Stuff the Nose and attach it to the Face with hidden stitches.

11. Stitch eye buttons in place with button and carpet thread, indenting the face slightly.

12. Attach the mustache (face fur), with hidden stitches or Sobo glue or both.

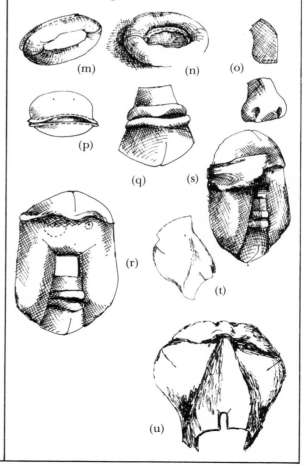

(m)   (n)   (o)

(p)   (q)   (s)

(r)   (t)

(u)

Head V (Furry)

1. Stitch center dart A, cheek darts B and C, and upper lip darts D.

2. Fold the Face right sides out. Match and stitch lines E to form the nose (t).

3. Cut 2 small cardboard discs to place behind the eyes on the wrong side of the fabric. Secure the eyes (brass-head paper fasteners in the example), to the Face and the cardboard backing.

4. Fold brow pleats F and secure them with a few small stitches over the eyes and the bridge of the nose (u).

5. Stitch the upper lip/under nose seam G.

6. Stuff the Nose area. Indent "nostrils" with a few small stitches at dots.

7. Fold the Lower Lip to stitch seam H.

8. Join the Lower Lip, Chin piece, and Upper Lip at seam I to the large dots.

9. Working from the back, stitch the Inner Mouth piece and foam backing to the inner edges of the Lips with Whip Stitch.

10. Attach Styrofoam "teeth" as in Head II, step 7.

11. Stitch the Ears around the outer edge. Turn them right side out, form pleats, and secure the pleats with top stitching.

12. Pin the Ears in position on the Face, raw edges together.

13. Stitch Head Back darts J and K.

14. Join the Head Back and Face around the outer edge, including the Ear margins in the seam, and leaving an opening between dots. Turn the Head right side out and stuff it.

Arms and Hands

1. Stitch the front and back of each Arm and Hand together. Turn the pieces right side out and stuff them.

2. Stitch, turn right side out, and stuff the Thumbs, and attach them to the Hands with hidden stitches.

3. Join the Hands and Arms, varying the gestures by the hand positions. Fold the raw edges inside and stitch with hidden stitches.

Cape

1. Hem the top edge for a drawstring.

2. Stitch Sleeve under-arm seams A. Insert the finished sleeves into the Cape armholes, and stitch seams B for set-in sleeves.

3. Position 3 Heads and the corresponding Arms for all 5 Heads on the Cape as desired with button and carpet thread, and large stitches from inside the Cape; large safety pins may also be used.

Legs and Feet

1. If there are to be toes, stitch, turn, and stuff them first.

2. Stitch the front and back seams of each Leg/Foot piece. Fold the seam onto itself to stitch the heel and toe darts across it, inserting finished toes (raw edges together) to include them in the toe darts.

3. Stuff the Legs and close the tops with top stitching.

4. Match the finished Legs to the corresponding Heads and Arms, and attach them to the wire ring (v) and to wearer's waist with fabric strips or cord tied to belt.

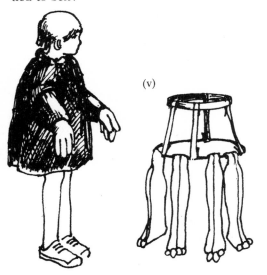

(v)

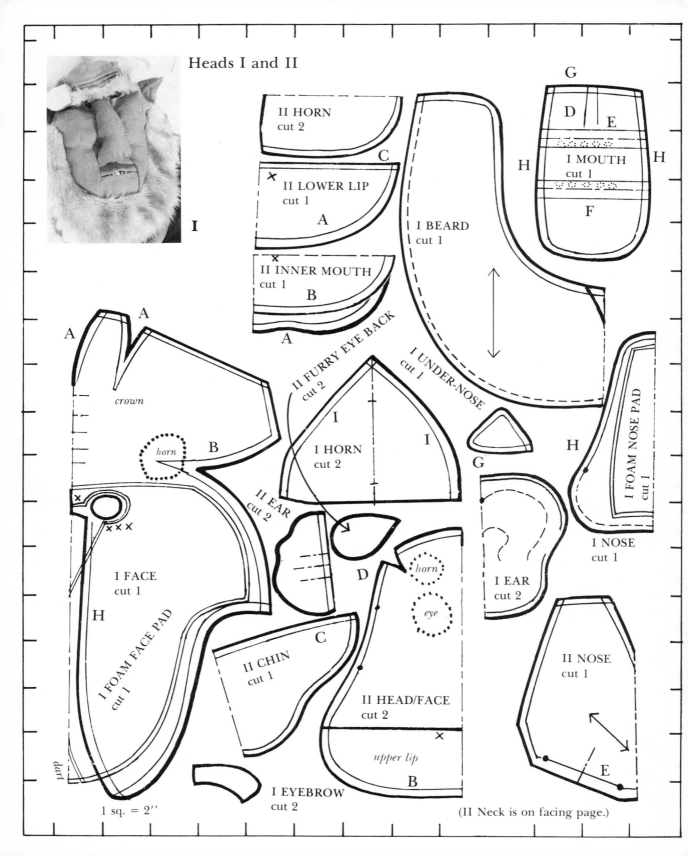

Heads I and II

II HORN
cut 2
C

II LOWER LIP
cut 1
A

II INNER MOUTH
cut 1
B

A

I BEARD
cut 1

G

D   E

I MOUTH
cut 1
H   H

F

II FURRY EYE BACK
cut 2

I UNDER-NOSE
cut 1

A   A

crown

horn

B

I HORN
cut 2
I   I

G

H

I FOAM NOSE PAD
cut 1

II EAR
cut 2

D

horn

I NOSE
cut 1

I FACE
cut 1

H

I FOAM FACE PAD
cut 1

eye

I EAR
cut 2

II CHIN
cut 1
C

II HEAD/FACE
cut 2

II NOSE
cut 1

E

dart

upper lip

B

I EYEBROW
cut 2

1 sq. = 2''

(II Neck is on facing page.)

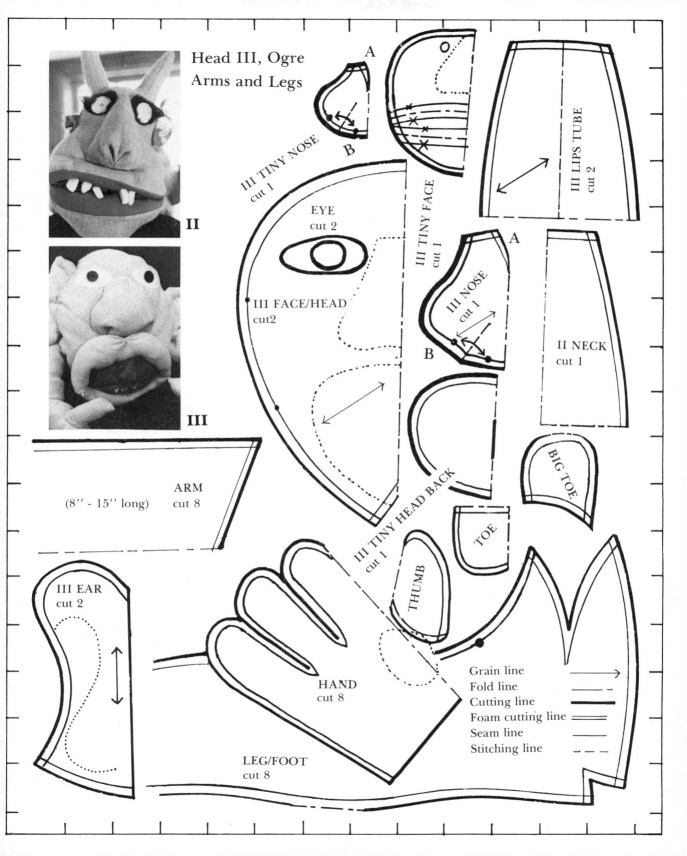

Head III, Ogre
Arms and Legs

II

III

III TINY NOSE
cut 1

A

B

III TINY FACE
cut 1

III LIPS TUBE
cut 2

EYE
cut 2

III FACE/HEAD
cut2

A

III NOSE
cut 1

B

II NECK
cut 1

III TINY HEAD BACK
cut 1

BIG TOE

TOE

THUMB

ARM
cut 8

(8″ - 15″ long)

III EAR
cut 2

HAND
cut 8

LEG/FOOT
cut 8

Grain line
Fold line
Cutting line
Foam cutting line
Seam line
Stitching line

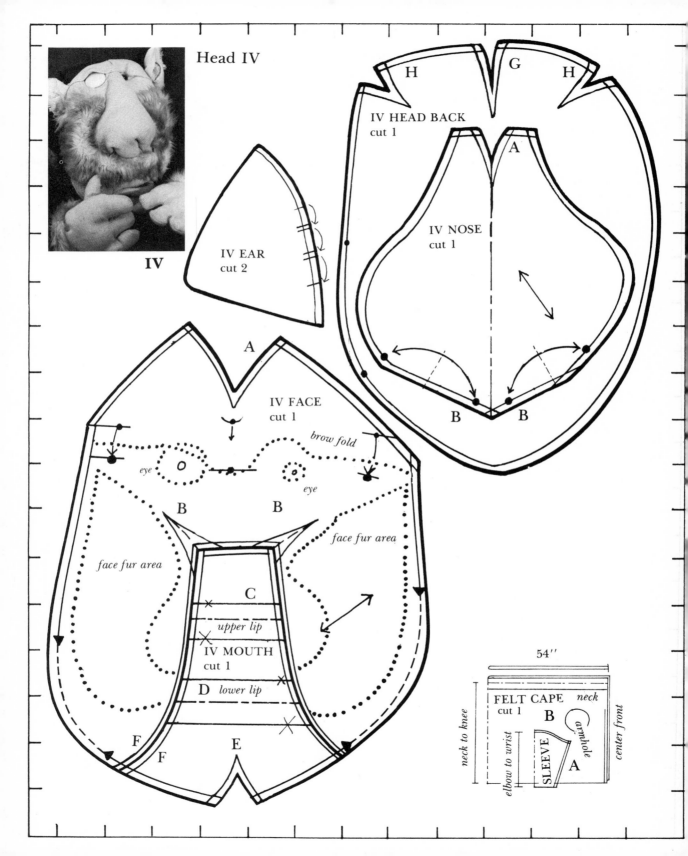

Head IV

IV

IV EAR
cut 2

IV HEAD BACK
cut 1

H   G   H

A

IV NOSE
cut 1

B   B

IV FACE
cut 1

A

brow fold

eye   eye

B   B

face fur area   face fur area

C

upper lip

IV MOUTH
cut 1

D lower lip

F   E
   F

54''

FELT CAPE
cut 1   neck

B

neck to knee

SLEEVE   A

elbow to wrist

armhole

center front

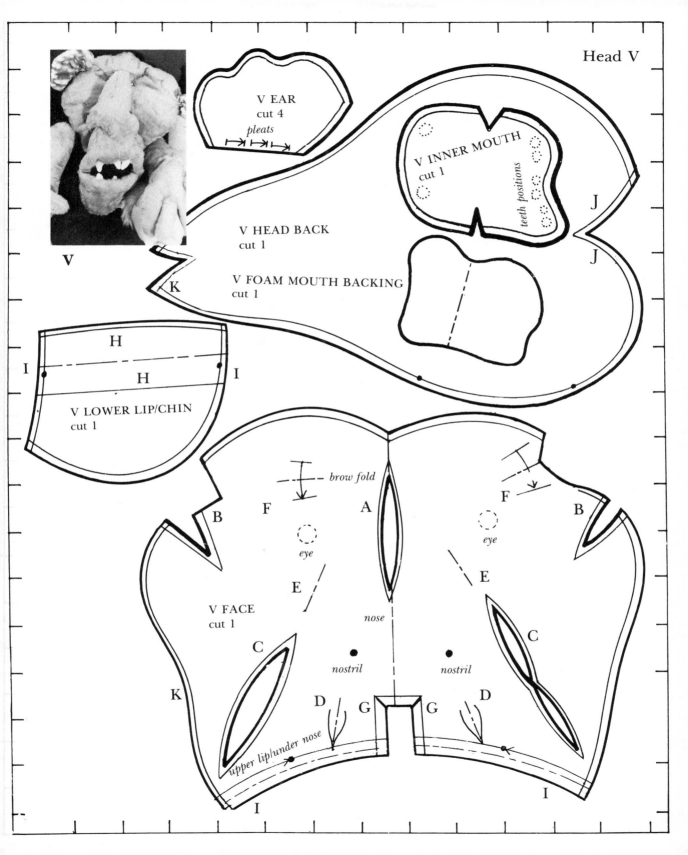

V EAR
cut 4
pleats

V INNER MOUTH
cut 1

teeth positions

J

J

V

V HEAD BACK
cut 1

V FOAM MOUTH BACKING
cut 1

K

H

H

I

I

V LOWER LIP/CHIN
cut 1

brow fold

F

A

F

B

B

eye

eye

E

E

V FACE
cut 1

C

C

nose

nostril

nostril

K

D

G

G

D

upper lip/under nose

I

I

Nonutilitarian Sewn Sculpture

HEN THE CRAFTSMAN begins a piece of work that is to have no useful purpose other than its aesthetic value, he is approaching art in the modern sense. Within the discipline of sewn sculpture, he either works against tremendous odds by endeavoring to overcome our personal reactions to or our familiarity with his medium and materials; or he turns these unavoidable aspects to his advantage. Perhaps the latter is best done through the use of forms to which the medium, his language, lends itself naturally: soft, representational forms; forms in which seams and roundness may be readily accepted; forms with subject matter that will offset the strong associations we have with the materials or that will be supported and enhanced by those associations.

Imagine a nonrepresentational sewn piece you might make — even one in which rounded forms are to play an important design role. With the forms already in your repertoire, this imaginary piece can be very exciting. Perhaps you can even picture the necessary stitching as highly decorative linear statements, disassociated from the needle-and-thread process we know. But what fabrics will you choose? You realize that we will think of breadsticks if you use red and white checks; we will think of winter, or of sheep, or of itching if you choose wool. We are apt to recall anything from baby blankets to hotel draperies, from Uncle Bob's golfing cap to Aunt Jemima's kerchief — you have lost control. The implications of the materials have confused the abstraction you meant to convey.

Imagine, instead, a representational piece of sewn sculpture — form and subject matter we can recognize. It does not have to be naturalistic, just recognizable. The subject is someTHING, not an art idea alone. Now visualize materials you might use; see how much more varied the selection becomes. Now a material can be so right for the subject as to be accepted without notice; or, by the fact that we are so familiar with it that we know it by feel, and by association with its many roles in our lives, it may exemplify the very quality of the subject you wish to emphasize.

Orphan Annie Doll

THIS DOLL (page 125) is not a plaything doll; it is an idea. It is an adaptation of a character from one popular medium to another. It is Pop Art. Whether or not we have ever sent for a decoder ring or named a dog Sandy, we know Orphan Annie. This doll is a three-dimensional symbol, which each of us reads a little differently.

The Orphan Annie Doll is 42 inches tall. She is made up of simple pillow forms assembled by hand. Her blank eyes and mouth are ironed on. The masses of curls are machine-stitched onto narrow bias strips, then glued into place.

Materials
½ yd. red cotton flannel for dress
½ yd. peach-colored cotton for head, neck, hands
¼ yd. white cotton for collar, cuffs, socks
¼ yd. black cotton for shoes
White iron-on mending cloth
2 lbs. polyester fiber
Curved upholstery needle
Heavy-duty thread
1 skein gold knitting worsted, 4 oz.
Peach or gold bias tape
Sobo or other fabric glue
24″ white grosgrain ribbon, 1″ wide
A black, permanent felt-tip marker

Directions
Note: All seams and darts are stitched right sides together unless otherwise noted.

Shoes, Socks, and Legs

1. Join the 2 sides of each Shoe at the front, stitching seam A to the toe dart C.

2. Join the 2 sides of each Sock at seam B.

3. Fold the raw edge of each Shoe top and Sock top to the wrong side and press. With right sides up, pin the pressed Shoe tops in position on the Socks, aligning center fronts. Top-stitch the Shoes to the Socks, making a Lapped Seam.

4. Top-stitch the pressed Sock tops to the Legs in the same manner (a).

(pattern appears on page 120.)

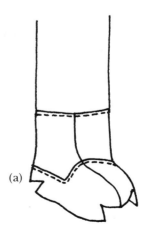

(a)

5. Continue stitching seams A to close the Shoes, Socks, and Legs.

6. Stitch toe darts C and heel darts D (across the A seams).

7. Stuff the Shoe, Sock, and Leg pieces.

Sleeves and Cuffs
8. Stitch each Cuff around the outer edge, leaving the wrist edge open. Clip the corner margins. Turn the Cuffs right side out and press them.

9. Making a Lapped Seam, top-stitch the finished Cuffs over the Sleeves, aligning the wrist (raw) edges (b).

Collar, Neck, and Dress
10. Stitch (separately) the Collar Front and Collar Back outer seams. Clip the corner and curved seam margins; turn and press as with the Cuffs.

11. Join the Neck Front and Dress Front with the Collar Front sandwiched between them (c). Join the Neck, Dress, and Collar backs in the same manner.

12. Join the Neck, Dress, and Collar Fronts and Backs at the shoulder and Neck seams E.

13. Join the Sleeves and Dress at seams F.

14. Join the Dress Front and Back and finish the arms with continuous under-arm and side seams from the wrist to the Dress hem Leg opening. Clip the under-arm seam margins and hem-corner margins.

15. Turn the Dress and Sleeves right side out through either the Neck or the Leg opening and stuff them.

Hands
16. Stitch on the outer seam line around each hand, leaving the wrist edge open. Clip the curved seam margins.

17. Turn the hands right side out and stuff them lightly. Machine top-stitch the fingers on the quilting lines.

18. Insert the Hands into the cuffed Sleeves. Pull the Cuffs down over the Hands. Attach the Hands to the Sleeves with Running Stitch, catching the

Cuff and Sleeve wrist margins in the stitching (d).

19. Wrap the grosgrain ribbon belt around the waist and secure it with a few stitches.

20. Attach the left Hand to the hip with a few hidden stitches.

Attach the Legs
21. Insert the finished Legs into the Leg opening and attach them with hidden stitches all around the Legs (e).

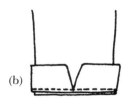

(b)

(c)

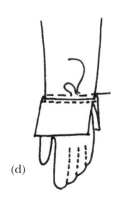

(d)

Head

22. Cut the eyes and mouth from iron-on mending fabric; outline them with a permanent marker and iron them onto the face.

23. Use a permanent marker to make nose marks on the face.

24. Join the Face and back of the Head around the outer seam line, leaving on opening between dots for turning and stuffing. Clip the curved seam margin, turn the Head right side out, and stuff it. Close the opening with Whip Stitch.

Join the Head and Neck

25. Use a curved upholstery needle and heavy-duty thread to stitch the Head to the Neck, folding the Neck raw edge to the inside as you stitch.

Hair

26. Make the curls in groups by wrapping knitting worsted around a 16″ – 18″-long strip of cardboard to make long loops. Lay the loops flat over 3″ – 6″-long strips of bias binding placed at 6″ intervals under the yarn loops (f).

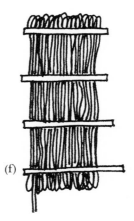

(f)

27. Stitch the yarn strands to the bias strips with very short machine stitches.

28. Arrange the groups of curls on the Head, pinning the bias strips about 1″ apart to make yarn loops (curls) between them (g). When the hair area is covered with curl groups, remove the pins as you glue each bias strip to the Head with Sobo glue.

(g)

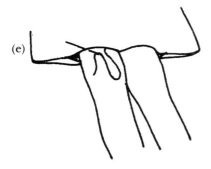

(e)

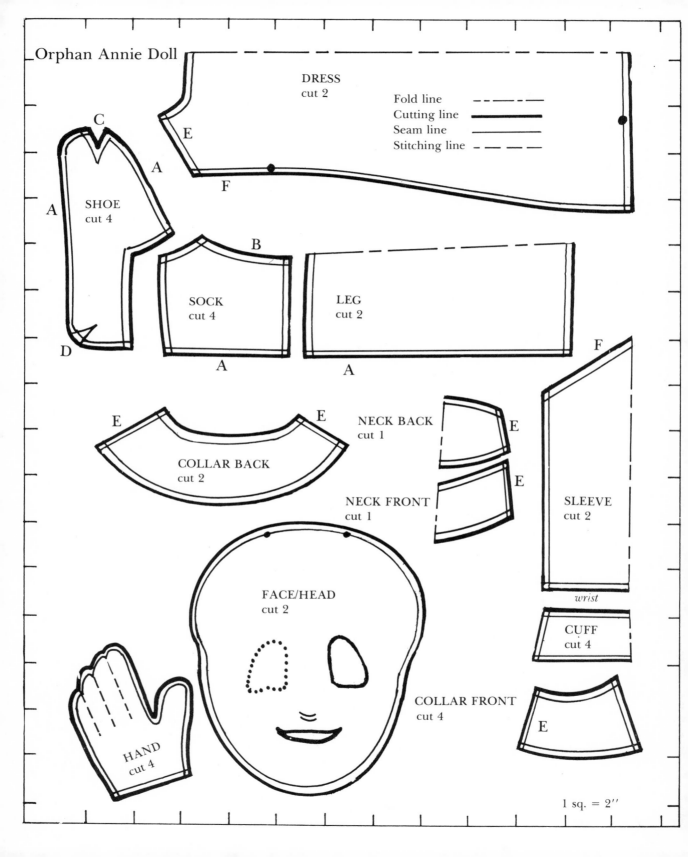

Art Nouveau Plant Form

 F COURSE, you won't make a piece exactly like the example (page 126), but if you wish to explore similar forms, the general directions below may be of help.

Materials

Natural Brazilian pigskin, approx. 20″ square
2 – 3-oz. tooling cowhide scraps totaling approx. 18″ square
Sharp shears
Objects to use as molds and temporary support for wet-shaping the leather
Omega leather dyes, medium brown and cordovan
Food colors, red and blue
Dye applicators or cotton balls and plastic gloves
Modeling tool with 1 spoon-shaped end, 1 tracer end
A few heavy rubber bands, spring-type clothespins, and pushpins
Rawhide mallet or substitute
Sobo glue
Leather finish and buffer
#3 glover's needle and polyester buttonhole twist or waxed linen thread

General Directions

Note: This piece was formed over a wooden support comprised of a platform with 2 dowels nailed to it from underneath (a). Construct a support as needed for your interpretation.

Rootstalk

1. Dye the pigskin and allow it to become nearly or completely dry. Then soak it in warm water for a few minutes. Remove it and, picking it up in the center, wring it (b), searching the wrinkles for likely growth forms.

2. Arrange the wet, wrinkled leather over the wooden support, securing it with pushpins and clothespins wherever necessary to retain the forms (c). You may cut out areas of leather to

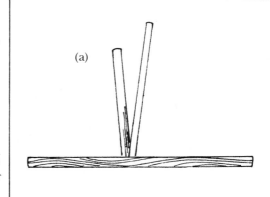

(a)

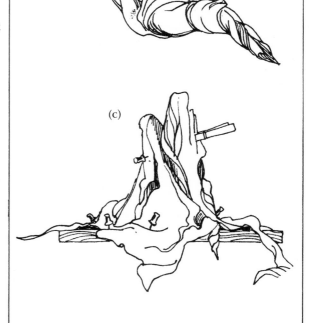

(b)

(c)

twist, loop, or even knot narrower end pieces (d). Forms may be refined and completed when the leather is dry, using glue or stitches.

3. If you're displeased with one arrangement, simply remove the pins and resoak the leather to begin again.

4. When you like your results, set the piece aside to dry — near warmth if stiffness is desired, as was the case with the example.

Buds
5. Using food colors, dye, dry, and soak the cowhide scraps. Wet-shape them over hard round forms of various sizes, such as knobs, wooden balls, and even Ping-Pong balls.

6. To make Buds such as those in the examples, fold the leather to make a dart over the form from one side to the center, diminishing the dart fold toward the center (e). Continue in this manner, making 5 darts. The spoon end of the modeling tool is of great help in creasing the folds (f).

7. Wrap the leather with a rubber band to secure it below the form (g). Using the modeling tool, make subtle creases and depressions in the rounded leather for the desired results. Allow the Buds to dry.

Calyxes
8. Cut Calyxes for the Buds from scraps of predyed 2-oz. cowhide.

9. Soak the Calyx pieces and wet-shape them with your fingers (h). Set them aside to dry.

Leaves
10. Soak predyed, precut Leaf shapes of tooling cowhide. Make accordion pleats in the stalk ends of the Leaves (i) and pound them with a mallet to make lasting creases. Secure the pleats with clothespins. Stretch the blade area of the Leaves with your fingers . Set the pieces aside to dry.

Finishing
11. Remove the clothespins and pushpins from the Rootstalk piece. Trim excess leather and glue or stitch the areas that require it.

12. You may wish to highlight areas of the Rootstalk, Buds, and Leaves with an application of a leather finish and buffing at this time.

13. Trim excess bulk from all the pieces to be joined, using a skiving knife (or safety beveler). Stuff the Buds with polyester fiber and glue or stitch them closed. Glue the buds to the Calyxes, the Calyxes and Leaves to the Rootstalk.

14. Remove from form.

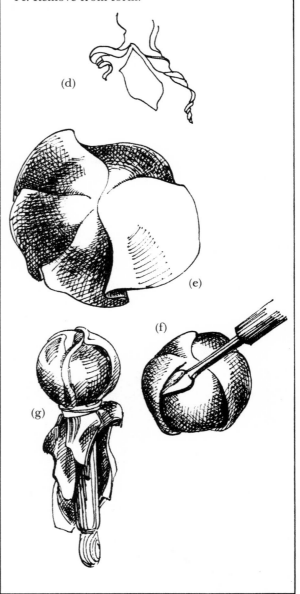

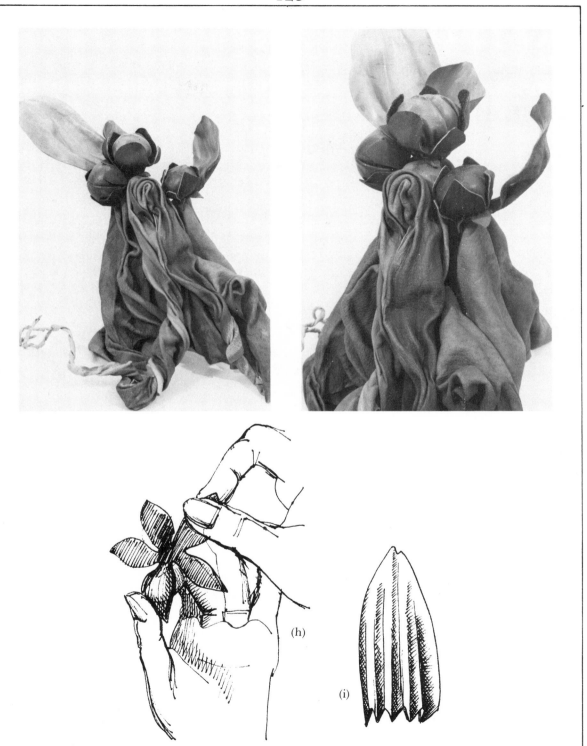

(h)

(i)

Gentlebeast

THIS CLOVEN-HOOFED composite of gazelle-like animals (page 127) was designed to grace a home with a reminder of some imaginary glade through subject matter, gesture, and the reminiscence of a sun-dappled woodland floor. It's a Gentlebeast to rest against or to stage as sculpture for the pleasurable feelings it may instill in those who encounter it. Its spiraled horns accent the subtly modeled bulk of its body, and its dark-amber-colored eyes are captivating. It is made of leather, wet-shaped and batiked. The hand stitching delineates the forms with the quality of drawing.

Materials

1 hide, reversible cowhide (6-oz., smooth, pliable leather)
Scrap of stiffer, 2-oz. or 3-oz. cowhide, 33″ × 12″ (for horns)
Edge creaser
#6 spacing wheel
Awl
3 or 4 spring-type clothespins
4 oz. Batik wax and leather batiking supplies (see pages 54, 55)
Omega dye, 8 oz. medium brown or 4 oz. each medium and light brown
4-oz. can rubber cement
2 amber-colored hard plastic beads, 1¼″ diam. (for eyes)
Fine sandpaper
2 oz. Sobo glue
#16 tapestry needle
Sailmaker's needle
Curved upholstery needle (optional)
4 oz. spool brown waxed linen thread
3 shopping bags of excelsior or wood shavings
10 lbs. polyester fiber
Tan Kote or other leather finish for a subtle sheen
Lamb's wool scraps or very soft cloth for buffing

General Directions

The entire Gentlebeast may be cut from one hide of leather, or, as with the example, the Neck, Face, Tail, and Hoofs may be cut from scraps of a natural-colored soft-tanned cowhide.
Note: Because of the shaping called for, this piece is not suitable for cloth.

Place the pattern pieces on the grain side of the leather utilizing the most pliable belly area for the Front Legs. The Flanks call for the most shaping, or stretching, and should be placed where shaping will be possible.

Trace around the pattern edges with an awl. Mark darts and pleats through the pattern with the point of the awl. Mark areas for shaping and any other information you'll need on the flesh side of the leather with a ball point pen.

Cut the leather with sharp shears, following the awl lines.

Mark all pieces for stitching holes with an edge creaser and spacing wheel. Whenever possible, join the 2 pieces, flesh sides together, with rubber cement along the seam margins to mark and punch stitching holes.

(pattern begins on page 134)

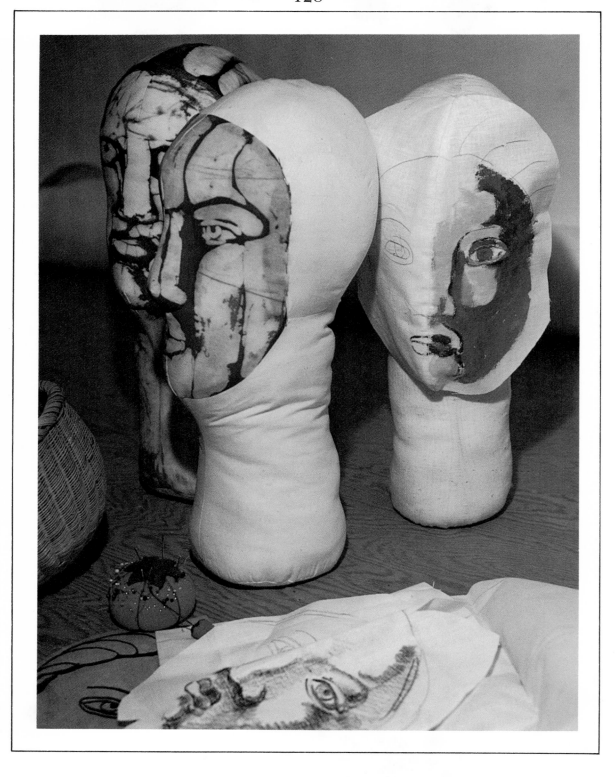

To join uncemented seams temporarily for stitching, use button and carpet thread and a Buttonhole Stitch, aligning every third or fourth hole on each side (a). This will show where, if at all, the seam must be eased or double-stitched to come out even.

Stitching from 2 holes on one side to one hole on the other side (b) results in a slight bulge on one side (X), helpful for shaping some areas.

Note: All seams may remain rubber-cemented together, or parted and restuck as convenient.

Punch the stitching holes before dyeing the leather, using an awl as described on page 53.

Wet-shaping is used to give added form to the Flanks, Outer Face nostril and eye areas, Ears, Tail, and the joint areas of the Legs. See page 52 for wet-shaping directions.

Batik the preshaped leather pieces according to the directions on page 55.

Stitch the seams with a tapestry needle and waxed linen thread. Each stitch must be pulled taut. For your comfort, make a leather finger sleeve to fit snugly around the first joint of the first finger of your stitching hand (c), or use a finger cut from an old kid glove. Leather will allow you to grip the waxed thread and will cushion your finger.

Form and join the individual parts of this piece in the order given here.

To prepare each piece for shaping and batiking, join dart seams marked with corresponding letters to punch stitching holes simultaneously. Punch pleat and dart stitching holes individually, counting the holes for correct alignment. Stitch dart seams that enter shaded (shaping) areas, and all pleats and darts. Stitch pleats and darts from the flesh side with Cobbler's Stitch or Back Stitch. Stitch dart seams from the grain side with Fishbone Stitch for Butt Seams. See the stitches on pages 50 and 51.

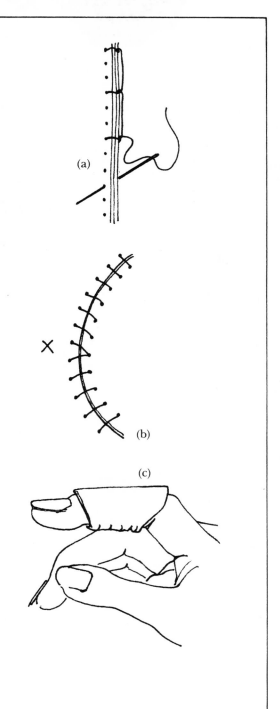

Directions for Forming Individual Pieces and for Assembly

Right Flank/Hind Leg

1. Join (with rubber cement), mark, and punch stitching holes and stitch dart seams A and F, pleats B and C, darts D and E, and tuck e. Mark and punch hoof edge G and flank edge I. Bend leg area to join, mark, and punch seam H.

2. Join center back seam J (Right and Left Flanks), to mark and punch stitching holes.

3. Separate seam H before wet-shaping the piece. Stitch after batiking, using Fishbone Stitch.

Left Flank (without a leg)

4. Join edges of flank dart K to mark, punch, and stitch. Use Fishbone Stitch, parting the rubber cement as you stitch.

5. Mark and punch flank edge I.

6. Wet-shape the piece.

Note: Batik both Flanks now or after stitching and stuffing.

Tail

7. Make stitching holes in the base of the Tail, then join the sides to mark and punch holes from the base to the dot.

8. Separate the sides before wet-shaping the Tail. Stitch after batiking, using Fishbone Stitch.

Join Right Flank to Left Flank

9. Stitch rump seam J from the top to the tail mark, forming a ridge with Whip Stitch. Separate rubber-cemented seam J below the Tail.

Attach Tail to Rump (Right and Left Flanks)

10. Hold the Tail in position on the finished part of rump seam J to mark corresponding stitching holes in the rump through the Tail holes; punch the holes. Stitch the Tail to the rump with the Joining Stitch (d).

11. Continue joining the Right Flank to the Left Flank below the Tail, stitching from the flesh side with Double Needle or Whip Stitch.

Body (Right and Left)

12. Mark and punch stitching holes around Leg holes P and Q. Join Right and Left pieces at center back seam M, and chest/belly seam N to mark and punch stitching holes.

13. Stitch seam M with Whip Stitch, forming a ridge.

14. Mark and punch curved Flank edge I and Neck edge O.

Note: Batik Body now or after stitching and stuffing.

15. Stitch chest/belly seam N from the Neck edge to the dot, with Fishbone Stitch.

Join Body and Flanks

16. Beginning at center back, use the temporary Buttonhole Stitch (a), to fit the finished Flanks to the Body at seam I, making double stitches as needed to give added fullness to the *Flank*. Stitch Flank seam I with Fishbone Stitch.

17. Close all but 9″ of belly seam N with Fishbone Stitch.

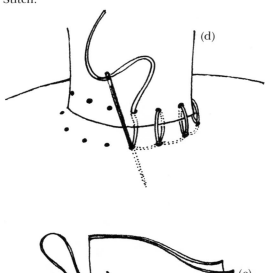

(d)

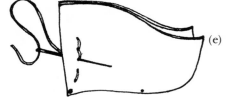

(e)

Front Legs (Right and Left)

18. Join dart seams A and F to mark, punch, and stitch with Fishbone Stitch.

19. Mark and punch shoulder edge Q, hoof edge G, pleats B, C, and D (and additional tuck in Right Front Leg). Punch pleat holes individually.

20. Bend the lower Leg to join edges R to mark and punch stitching holes.

21. Separate edges R to wet-shape as indicated on the pattern.

Note: Batik Front Legs while flat. Stitch pleats B, C, and D on the flesh side with Cobbler's or Back Stitch after batiking. Stitch darts A and F, and seams R with Fishbone Stitch.

22. Stuff the Right Leg slightly and stitch the tuck to bend the leg. Knot the thread and conceal it in the fold. Work from the outside, catching a little batting in the stitches. Pull the stitches taut for a good fold. Stuff both legs moderately just above the hoofs, densely at the "joints."

Hoofs

23. Mark and punch stitching holes for open dart H. Stitch on the flesh side with Cobbler's Stitch (e).

24. Mark and punch stitching holes in Leg edge G.

25. Fold flesh sides together, bringing the small dots to the large center dot on the bottom edge (f). Rubber-cement the bottom edge to itself. Mark and punch holes, and stitch with Fishbone Stitch.

26. Stuff "cloven" area of Hoof firmly with excelsior.

Attach Hoofs to Legs

27. Matching *'s, join each Hoof and Leg at seams G with Whip Stitch.

Attach Front Legs to Body

28. Stitch the Left Front Leg to Leg hole Q, the Right Front Leg to Leg hole P, using the Joining Stitch (d).

Neck

29. Join back-of-Neck edges S to mark, punch, and stitch with Whip Stitch to form a ridge.

30. Mark and punch stitching holes in Neck edge O, head edge U, and lower Neck edge T.

Note: Batik the Neck while it's flat.

31. Stitch the Lower Neck seam T with Fishbone Stitch.

Attach Neck to Body

32. Use Fishbone Stitch to join the Body and Neck seams O.

Ears

33. Follow Tail directions to form Ears in the same manner, making one right and one left Ear.

34. Stuff the base of each Ear with a leather-scrap-covered wad of batting, secured with Sobo glue (g).

(f)

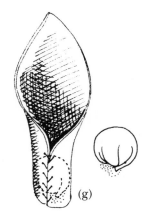

(g)

Horns

Note: if the Horns are to be dyed, do so before shaping.

35. Wet the Horn pieces and shape them as follows: tightly curl the small end toward the flesh side·of the leather, aligned with the edge of the Horn marked *top* (h). Continue curling from the tip downward, forming a spiral. (The *top* edge will remain visible the length of the spiral.) Secure the spiral at the base of the horn with a clothespin and allow it to dry completely.

36. Lightly mark the exact overlap, tracing along the *top* edge of the spiral with an awl. Remove the clothespin to open out the spiral. Roughen the grain side of the overlap edge with fine sandpaper so glue will adhere to it.

37. Mark and punch stitching holes at the base of the Horn and at the spiral's final overlap.

38. Apply glue to the flesh side of the *top* edge. Carefully re-spiral the Horn from the tip to the base, following the awl lines. Allow the glue to dry thoroughly.

39. Whip-stitch the final overlap. Stuff the Horns.

Outer Face

40. Mark and punch stitching holes around outer edge to the x. (The edges of the nostrils remain unpunched.)

41. Fold the Outer Face to form dart I, tiny seam J, and outer edges of the nostrils, to mark and punch stitching holes.

42. Stitch seam J and dart I between the large and small dots with Fishbone Stitch.

43. Wet-shape as indicated on the pattern; crease and curve the nostrils and stretch the brow into mounds (without distorting the outer edges).

Attach Ears and Horns to Outer Face

44. Holding each Ear or Horn in position on the Outer Face, mark stitching holes corresponding to those in the punched pieces. Punch the holes, and attach the Ears and Horns with the Joining Stitch (d).

Face (Head)

45. Join dart K and seam W to mark and punch stitching holes. Mark and punch neck edge U.

46. Stitch dart K (hidden later).

47. Stitch seam W (to the dot), with Fishbone Stitch.

48. Wet-shape the piece as indicated; shape the eye areas over round forms such as tennis balls, packing the face with paper shreds to secure the forms while the leather dries.

49. Separate the cemented section of seam W. Position Outer Face on Face, aligning the top edges. Temporarily join them with dabs of rubber cement.

50. Mark and punch corresponding stitching holes on the face along the edge of the Outer Face and nostrils.

Note: Batik the Face and Outer Face.

51. Use the Joining Stitch to attach the Outer Face to the Face, leaving the top (behind the Horns), unstitched.

52. Stitch seam W with Fishbone Stitch.

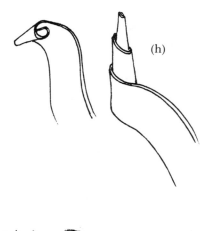

(h)

Insert Eyes

53. Wet-shape the eye holders, using the eyes as forms. When dry, clip notches in the ruffled edges of the leather (i). If the eyes are beads, secure them to the eye holders with a few stitches; if not, use Sobo glue to hold them in place.

54. Glue the eye holders in position behind the eye holes.

55. Stuff the Face firmly. Stuff the space between the Outer Face and Face lightly down the bridge of the nose, and very firmly beneath the Horns.

Stuff the Gentlebeast

56. Stuff Right Flank and Hind Leg first, through the belly opening. Pack all shaped areas firmly with batting. For weight and density, pack a hard central core of excelsior in the body, surrounding it with a thick layer of firmly packed batting. Stuff the Rump, Left Flank, and Body (in that order), filling out the belly as the seam is stitched.

57. Continue stuffing through the Neck opening, adding a hard core of excelsior in the Neck. Stuff the Neck to overflowing, packing it firmly as the final seam joining the Head and Neck is stitched.

Attach Head to Neck

Note: Stitching behind the Horns and Ears is awkward. A curved upholstery needle will help.

58. Position the Head at an angle on the Neck (to the beast's right) for a more lifelike gesture. Temporarily secure the Head with a few stitches at intervals around the Neck. Stitch with Fishbone Stitch.

Finishing

59. Apply Tan Kote or other leather finish to protect and preserve the leather. Buff with a scrap of lamb's wool.

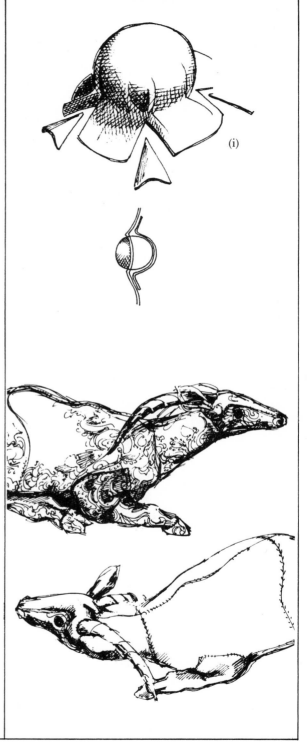

(i)

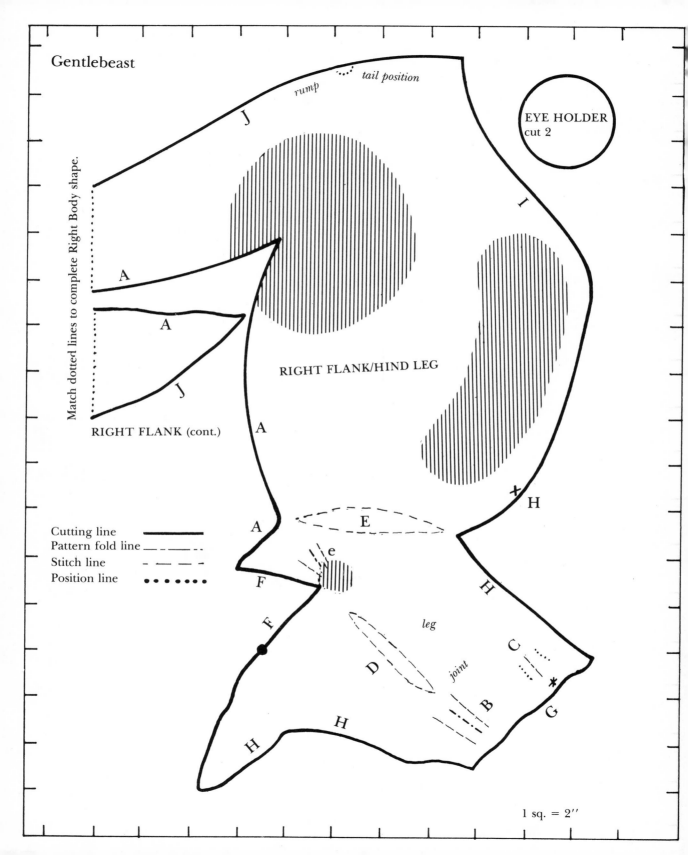

Gentlebeast

EYE HOLDER
cut 2

rump   *tail position*

J

Match dotted lines to complete Right Body shape.

A

A

J

RIGHT FLANK (cont.)

RIGHT FLANK/HIND LEG

I

A

H

A

E

A

e

F

H

F

leg

C

D

joint

B

G

H

H

Cutting line
Pattern fold line
Stitch line
Position line

1 sq. = 2''

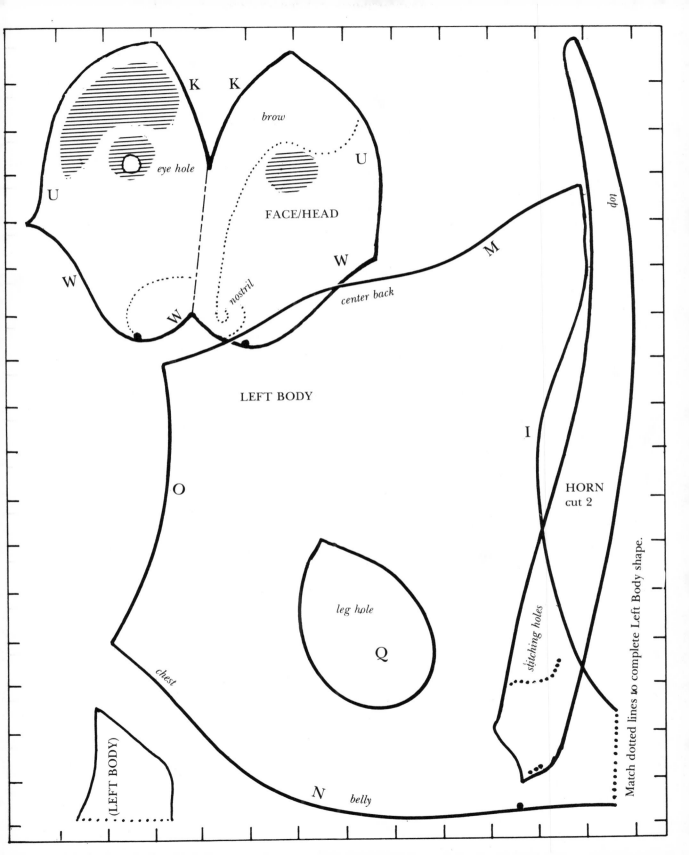

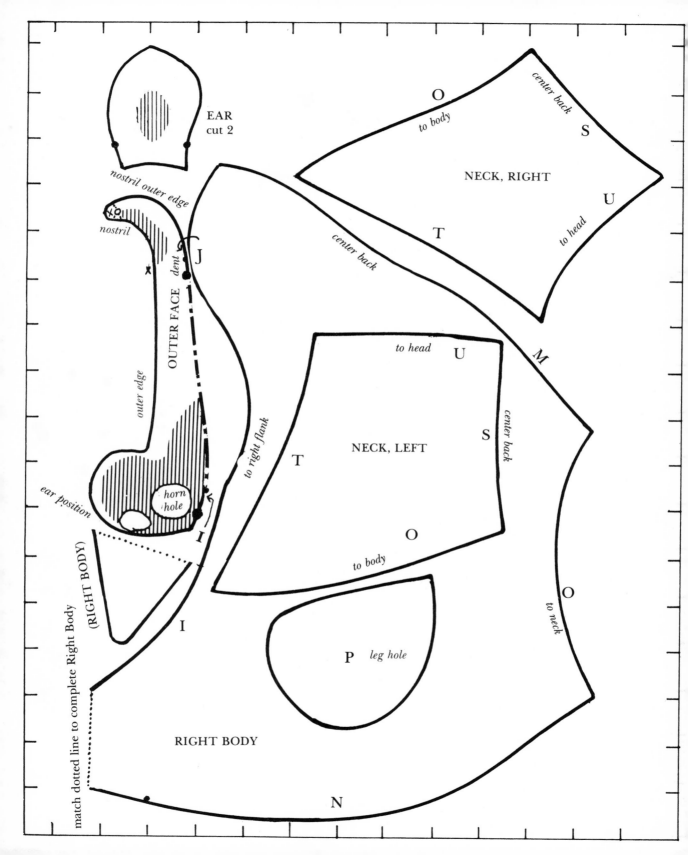

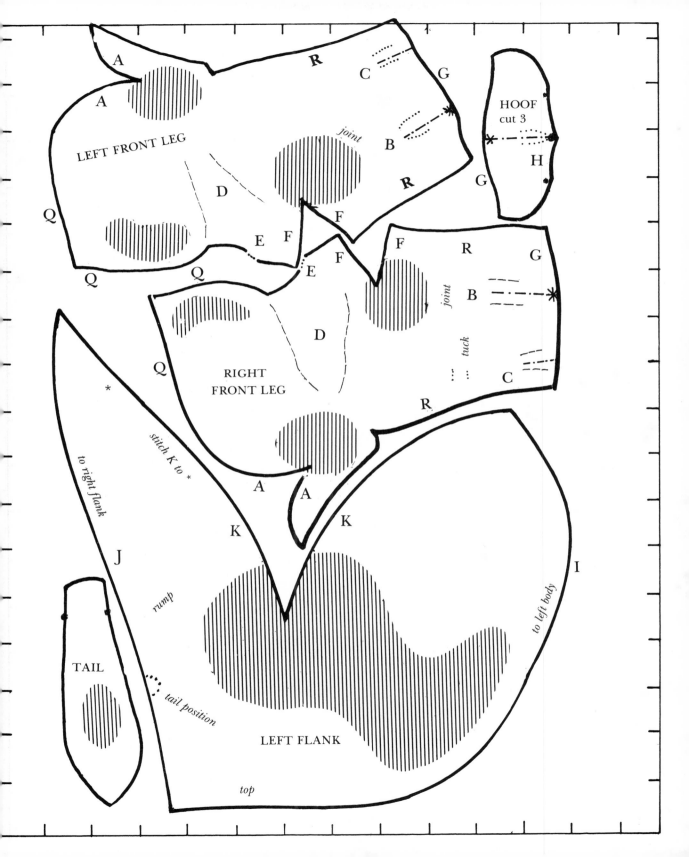

The Head

BEGINNING ON YOUR OWN soft sculpture design for the first time may raise the questions: "What can I make, and where will I start?" So, to postpone that dilemma for one more project, here is a start for you: a face shape, a neck, and a skull cap. See what you can do with it.

Think for a moment of a finished piece for an audience of one — you. What are your ideas about the human head, if it is to be human, and how do your ideas relate to this sculptural medium?

Change the basic forms as necessary to support your concept. There are a variety of head forms to borrow: baby caps, helmets, extraordinary hair shapes, elaborate headdresses, turbans. Or perhaps this concept will be one of animal or demonic forms or of artistic ideas. Consider embellishments: needlepoint, embroidery, acrylic paint, permanent markers, pencil, silk screen, batik, beadwork. You might knit or crochet a covering, or mask the basic forms in tooled, stamped, embroidered, or dyed leather.

Add sculptural features: add a hand shape, a stuffed glove perhaps — and the potential is expanded.

Look at the works of other artists and craftsmen of our own and other cultures for their ideas and treatments of the human head. Explore your own ideas, reactions, fascinations. Look at heads; look at masks.

Just a few of the endless possibilities are indicated in these sketches and in the unfinished examples on page 128. I wish I could see your results.

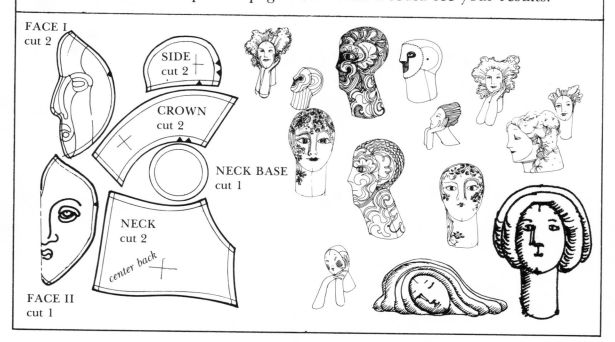

FACE I
cut 2

SIDE
cut 2

CROWN
cut 2

NECK BASE
cut 1

NECK
cut 2

center back

FACE II
cut 1

Exploring the Medium Further

EXPERIMENTATION IS the leading edge of any field of endeavor. Contrary to popular belief, students, with the possible exception of the very gifted, are unable to carry out meaningful experiments within their field. Enthusiasm is a great tool, but without experience, knowledge, and a little talent, it does not enable a person to attain new heights. Knowledge of the craft, gained only through experience, gives a basis for experimentation — to result in ideas and concepts beyond those common in the craft. Talent provides the delightful bonus of creative thinking: the ability to assemble the knowledge and the skills gained in experience and to take the next logical step with all these elements.

Exploration, on the other hand, is the student's realm. To explore with diligence, and in depth, media and methods within a discipline is to learn the limitations of that craft and oneself.

"Making a piece, any piece, is like looking into a mirror; it objectifies your feelings and your knowledge." – Morris Knight

Designing Sewn Sculpture

THE MAJOR PART of the time spent producing sewn sculpture is spent in designing. If you were to ask me how long it took me to make any of the examples you see here, the answer would perhaps surprise you if it did not include design time, and astound you if it did.

I usually explore an idea through sketches, trying to visualize the forms and where seams and other construction devices must be placed for structural and aesthetic purposes. These early studies for shell pillows illustrate some of my sketch-stage thinking. At this point, I am looking for similarities between the subject matter and the medium and investigating structural solutions. When the shapes I envision become too complicated for me to understand clearly through drawings, I take the next step with cloth, trying a rough pattern.

Note: The ability to draw is not a prerequisite of this sculptural craft. Even the best drawings can be misleading.

A good way to visualize a three-dimensional form is to model it in clay, either Plasticine (a nonhardening, oil-base clay), or a kiddie dough self-hardening material. In developing the Gentlebeast (page 127), I began with a small clay model. I needed to see the asymmetric forms of an animal resting with one hind leg underneath the body. My great Dane was the original model, along with zoo animals and photographs.

You began designing your own sewn sculpture with your first interpretation of a pattern from this book, if not before, and gained experience with each subsequent piece you made. And now, in order to bring your concepts to sewn sculpture in pieces of entirely your own design, you will want to make patterns from existing forms, from photographs, or from your imagination.

The Importance of Seams

The placement and types of seams are of primary importance to sewn sculpture. A seam may call attention to a textural or color change or to the design of a form, or it may be a line — a visual path or a barricade between two points. A seam that is unusually or illogically placed is conspicuous and must work to the decided advantage of the sculpture. A seam that is elaborately stitched is more noticeable than the simple seam inconspicuously joining two parts. Emphasis on a detail such as a seam generally calls attention to details throughout the sculpture.

Darts are less conspicuous since their effect appears at the apex, or beyond the stitching rather than parallel to it, and the stitching is usually hidden in the shadow of the larger form it creates. A darted head shape, for example, provides a form without interruption from a center seam. The addition of a darted nose makes the linear statement (seams), only where it is most widely accepted by our familiarity with drawing, with photography, and with real facial creases — at abrupt planar changes. The final effect is a face almost without seams. Now the concept is not hampered by our constant awareness of the medium or of the craft of sewing. Darts are used in place of full seams in many of the designs in this book.

Because we are accustomed to clothing seams, many sewn sculpture seams are acceptable to the point of invisibility. A seam on one side of a tubular form, for example, so closely resembles a sleeve seam that it is accepted as a matter of fact. To take an example from high fashion, the designer who molds a lace shoulder in a gown is calling attention to the form (the shoulder), and to the lace design by not destroying either. The seam follows the lace pattern, wrapping over and around the shoulder rather than visually cutting it into a front and back by the use of a central seam. It is a painstaking hand operation and naturally sets his work above any mass-produced piece — consideration for form is as important in one sculptural discipline as another.

Borrowing Shapes from Objects and Beings

To take a pattern from a three-dimensional form, you may be able to draw directly on the subject, designating the logical placement of seams based on changes in planes, colors, and textures and on linear details that apply to your use of the form. There are many possibilities in all but the simplest forms; that's the fun and the challenge to the designer.

Wrap and pin a piece of muslin over the subject, cutting the cloth as necessary. Draw the seam lines on the muslin, adding gathers, pleats, and/or darts to duplicate the form.

Remove the muslin pattern and clarify the drawn shapes. Cut, pin, and stitch the muslin pattern, and stuff the piece to see your results. Pin and mark areas that need alterations. Remove the stuffing and make the changes.

Continue in this manner until your trial pattern produces the form you set out to make. Mark all final seam lines and construction details with a colored marker to avoid confusion. Rip out the stitching again, iron the muslin pattern, and trace the shapes on paper for enlarging or reducing as required.

Borrowing Shapes from Patterns

To make a pattern without a guide subject, you may be able to use existing patterns as points of departure, as with The Head (page 138). Place a likely pattern on muslin. Cut the pattern and slide the pieces to expand or diminish particular areas. Draw additions or extensions directly on the muslin. Use a tape measure to make corresponding seams the same length. Test your muslin trial pattern as described above.

Beware: If a pattern you design produces a form which, however lovely, is not right for your concept, stop and evaluate the situation. If you can truly accept the new dictates created by the pattern, changing your concept to work with the pattern, by all means do so. But if you try to apply your original concept to a form that has taken on an entirely different mood or character, you are almost certain to end up with neither this nor that — in the dreaded middle. It would be better to file the pattern away and pursue your original concept. Producing a good pattern is never a wasted effort.

Materials as a Point of Departure

Often, when the urge to work precedes any definite idea, fingering through the materials of your craft is all the stimulus you need. A swirl of cloth or leather folds, soft and crisp finishes, prints and textures together, illusions of other substances you must touch to disprove, brilliant color, woven subtleties, and the instant memories of all your fondest associations with the materials are there for the rediscovery.

Although I feel that geometric and mechanical forms are the least suited to this medium, I realize you may wish to investigate their possibilities. Furniture, for example, may require shapes with a certain degree of flatness and with squared corners; and soft sculpture, reflecting the concern of fine art of the past twenty years, has dealt extensively with incongruities: soft machines, utensils, and vehicles, and stuffed food products are the most obvious examples.

If the inherent rolypoly quality of soft-edged forms is to be avoided, fabric abstractions of geometric or mechanical inspiration, for other than ironic statements, may require the use of stiffening agents in the materials or the stuffing, or super structures beneath the fabric shell, such as plastic or wire screening, wood armatures, buckram or horsehair materials, and wire. And, of course, the use of armatures has its place in cloth translations of natural growth forms, to support a large piece, to provide sharp contrast to the softness of the medium, or to add the element of mobility to a piece. Flexible wire gives this humorous Bumpkin doll movable lips and extremities.

A Word on "Doing Contemporary Work"

Why is it that none of the dolls created at the turn of the century resemble the little girls of today? Many little girls of the 1960s looked like Mattel's Chatty Cathy doll modeled after a little southern California girl of that time. I, myself, once resembled a Shirley Temple doll (1936); there were thousands of us. We knew, unawares, the subtleties of social form which made us walk and talk and look like little girls should — like Shirley Temple, our model, who was modeled after the beliefs of our parents' world. Little girls don't change, but our little girls don't see what we saw in a Shirley Temple doll.

Some crafts people strongly urge fellow enthusiasts to "do contemporary work," which I feel warrants mention here, lest you confuse anything in this book with that misleading advice. It is impossible for you to do anything other than contemporary pieces, and it would be a mistake to abandon your unique concepts in favor of attempts at something vaguely termed contemporary. Your every conception is a product of your time, as are your materials and attitudes toward your craft. You may do pieces which are reminiscent of, or copies of work of other periods, but your perceptions of those periods and of the work you copy are without benefit of the subtleties, which were common knowledge to those who lived then.